W9-BQM-233

THE ADVAITIC THEISM OF THE BHĀGAVATA PURĀṆA

The Advaitic Theism of THE BHĀGAVATA PURĀṆA

DANIEL P. SHERIDAN

ST. JOSEPH'S UNIVERSITY
3 9353 00239 2577

BL
1140.4
B437
S54
1986

MOTILAL BANARSIDASS
DELHI VARANASI PATNA MADRAS

First Edition 1986

MOTILAL BANARSIDASS
Bungalow Road, Jawahar Nagar, Delhi 110 007
Branches
Chowk, Varanasi 221 001
Ashok Rajpath, Patna 800 004
120 Royapettah High Road, Madras 600 004

© MOTILAL BANARSIDASS

ISBN: 81-208-0179-2

This project was supported in part by the Academic Grant Fund of Loyola University of New Orleans.

PRINTED IN INDIA
BY JAINENDRA PRAKASH JAIN AT SHRI JAINENDRA PRESS, A-45 NARAINA INDUSTRIAL AREA, PHASE I, NEW DELHI 110 028 AND PUBLISHED BY NARENDRA PRAKASH JAIN FOR MOTILAL BANARSIDASS, DELHI 110 007

In memory of

NORMAN KAMINSKI AND
WILLIAM SHERIDAN

FOREWORD

The *Bhāgavata Purāṇa* is a scripture superbly written, with aesthetic sensitivity, devotional intensity and metaphysical subtlety; a tapestry resplendent in its color, its intertwining motifs and its dancing figures, therein expressing a universe in which the divine and created worlds differentiate and identify in an endless sequence of mutual transformations. If much of this scripture is presented in long discursive passages and in overdrawn narratives, it culminates in the luxuriant world of Kṛṣṇa, the warrior-charioteer of the *Bhagavad Gītā* become the divine lover of the cowherd maidens.

The Kṛṣṇa legends are presented in a village folk setting with trickster episodes and erotic love-play that communicate some of the most distinctive aspects of the devotional traditions of India. Such a saviour personality ! A divine child who steals butter and plays pranks with his family, a youth who steals the garments of the maidens while they are swimming, who hides and then reveals himself, who dances with erotic delight with the village women, and in all this makes the divine present in its supreme transforming power. While such legends of an incarnate deity offend our western sense of divine dignity, they establish in India an archetypal figure that has inspired the religious life there in an all-pervasive manner over these many years. Indeed these are not merely fanciful tales; they are supported by the elaborate sequence of narrative recitations, descriptive passages and intellectual discourse. This is what gives to the *Bhāgavata Purāṇa* not only its amazing power over the emotions and sensitivities of India but also over its high intellectual perceptions.

That this *Purāṇa* should have been neglected for such a long period by the scholarly traditions of the west is not entirely surprising since the course of our studies has followed generally the course of the tradition itself by being centered first on the *Vedas*, the *Upaniṣads*, the *Epics*, the *Sūtras* and their commentaries. Yet the entire tradition was reshaped during the purāṇic period. The realities of India's religious life for the last thousand years must be understood under the influence of these theistic traditions that emerged in this time and in the light of intense devotionalism that resulted in both the Vaiṣṇava and in the Śaivite traditions. With such works as the *Rāmacaritamānasa* and the *Gīta Govinda* and the other devotional writings of the various vernacular languages a new religious world came into being that is much less understood by western scholars than the earlier components of the tradition.

So too with the *Bhāgavata Purāṇa*; its devotionalism tends to indicate to the modern mentality that it is lacking in intellectual subtlety or even that it is not of intellectual significance, that it does not deserve the attention lavished on some of the other writings of the tradition. That this is not so can be clearly seen in this study. This *Purāṇa* rivals in its insight and in the abundance of its memorable phrases the finest passages from any of the other masterworks of the tradition. To combine such depth of intellectual discourse with such heightened emotional resonance and such exciting imagery is a special genius of India. The heightened emotion becomes essential for the understanding while understanding that does not evoke intense emotional responses can hardly be accepted as authentic insight.

What is important just now is the elaboration of this tradition not only for India and its peoples but for the religious heritage of the human community. Each person is now the heir to the total human tradition as well as to the particular cultural and religious traditions of a particular region of the earth. The Kṛṣṇa stories and the associated religious thought belong to the realm of religious literature of the larger human community as do the Jātaka stories of Gotama Buddha and the biblical stories and even the stories of the tribal peoples of the various continents. Only when these come together can we appreciate the richness of the revelatory experience whereby the divine has communicated itself to the human community. Precisely because each of these has its own distinctive meaning and context of interpretation they are able to enrich each other.

The special contribution of India is its sensitivity to the presence of the divine within the phenomenal world. The lavish religious-cultural heritage of India can be considered as discovering ever more profound ways in which we are able not only to intellectually perceive the divine within the world of natural forms but also to participate in the divine activities themselves.

We live presently in the historic moment when our scientific inquiries into the innermost structure and functioning of the natural world are recovering our primordial intuitions of the numinous presence manifesting itself throughout the universe. That this experience has a shamanic quality has been recognized by the scientist, Brian Swimme, in his remarkable statement concerning the scientist in relation to these earlier forms of spiritual experience as well as to the classical religious cultures whose contemplative saints spent their lives in retirement and contemplation and then returned to speak to the people on the ultimate questions that concern themselves and the universe about them : "It is this same sense of ultimacy that the scientist has discovered in a profound encounter with the real, this same sense of the fantastic, the extraordinary, the real." By the very force of his inquiry the scientist finds himself assuming a trans-scientific role, a role similar to that carried out in former times "by the shaman or the contemplative recluse" (Teilhard Perspective, July, 1983). Science is truly the yoga of the west.

Thus the authors of the *Bhāgavata Purāṇa* in ancient times in India and the scientist in modern America find that they are finally involved in a similar project, an appreciation of the ultimate dynamics of the universe. Both are forced ultimately to a numinous sense of the universe as music or as dance. This we find directly stated by Leonard Feldstein in the title of his book, *The Dance of Being* and in a further statement of Brian Swimme that : "The fireball at the beginning of time is a huge molten ball ringing with music" (Creation, July/August, 1986, p. 25).

While the meeting of these two traditions is still in its incipient phase it is important that these traditions each continue on true to the arc of their own inner development. We can be assured that each will find a resonance and amplification in the other, both in the conscious and in the unconscious realms of the human psyche. Through this study of Daniel Sheridan the profound expression of India's experience as contained in the *Bhāgavata Purāṇa* is now available to us as never before. He is a gracious writer, a thinker through whom the meaning of the sacred text becomes available to us and will ring in our minds throughout the future with a new depth of appreciation.

July, 1986 THOMAS BERRY
Riverdale Center of Religious Studies,
New York.

CONTENTS

Chapter I

INTRODUCTION

The problem of the transcendence and immanence of the Divine has challenged the religious imagination of humankind from the moment men first began to consider their place in the universe. The variety of the solutions to this problem in the higher thought traditions is itself a dimension of the problem fascinating for the historian because it suggests that diversity is not in conflict with unity. Each tradition has an irreducible contribution to make toward a satisfactory solution of the relation of God and human. Whether to be distinguished from God or to be identified with God, whether God is near or far, are dilemmas which face the human in the intimate moments of interior anguish and in the public moments of community worship. The origins of the solutions are lost in the unrecorded attempts at self-understanding of early history. One form of solution has endured in India for the most of three millennia. Non-dualism surfaced in the speculations of the Upaniṣadic sages and ever since has been the context in which religious thinkers in India have formulated their visions. Such an enduring tradition has an important claim upon anyone who considers whether God is transcendent to or immanent in his universe.

Yet non-dualism can cut across a rigid dichotomy between transcendence and immanence. A God who is not ultimately different from the individual self transcends the limitations of specificity, individuality and temporality. A God who is not different from creatures is immanent in the forms evolving out of the divine self. A God who is not subject to time need not be distinguished from creatures on account of priority. Such a non-dualism seeks a 'both/and' solution to the problem of the transcendence and immanence of God in relation to creation. If a religious visionary beholds God in a preeminently personal form and has at the same time a profound conviction of God's identity with self and the universe, then a truly creative religious moment has occurred. Such a moment occurred in the ninth century in South India among the Brahmans who composed the *Bhāgavata Purāṇa*.[1] The *Bhāgavata*'s breadth of vision, profundity of insight, and untroubled philosophical naivete allow the historian to witness a great system of belief grappling with the perennial problem of God's transcendence and immanence.

The Bhāgavata Purāṇa

The scholar and the devout villager in India have looked to the *Bhāgavata Purāṇa* for guidance, vision, ecstasy, and the truth. Its first verse proclaims: "the True, the Supreme, on Him we meditate."[2] The *Bhāgavata* is considered the Fifth *Veda*, the greatest *Purāṇa* which, as Daniel H. H. Ingalls says, "stands out by reason of its literary excellence, the organization that it brings to its vast material, and the effect that it has had on later writers."[3] Three Vaiṣṇava schools, founded by Madhva, Vallabha, and Caitanya, view its teachings as authoritative. It is the main channel through which the stories and legends about Kṛṣṇa have entered the length and breadth of Hindu civilization. Yet in modern times the *Bhāgavata* has been either neglected or misunderstood by scholars of religion in the West. The systematics of the later *ācāryas* attracts the scholars' attention while the *Bhāgavata*'s encyclopedic inclusivity of Vaiṣṇava philosophy, theology, piety, and lore bewilder the modern gaze. Some of its tenets even repel

1. The *Bhāgavata Purāṇa* or *The Scripture of the Devotees of Bhagavān* is one of the eighteen great *Purāṇas*, which characterize the new sectarian Hinduism (1st millennium A.D.). A *Purāṇa* is an 'ancient thing,' a popular scripture of encyclopedic scope.

2. *Bhāgavata Purāṇa* I.1.1d : satyaṃ paraṃ dhīmahi// (This and all the following references to the *Bhāgavata Purāṇa* will be indicated by number alone. The translation, unless otherwise indicated, will be based on that of Tagare. The Sanskrit will be from the edition of 1983 by J. L. Shastri.

3. Daniel H. H. Ingalls, "Foreword," in *Krishna : Myths, Rites, and Attitudes*, ed. by Milton Singer (Chicago : University of Chicago Press, 1968), p. vi.

the secular scholar who searches it "from the strictly philosophical point of view," but, as S. Dasgupta reluctantly concedes, "it will be impossible to ignore the religious pathology that is associated with the devotional philosophy which is so predominant in the South and which so much influenced the minds of the people not only in the Middle Ages but also in the recent past and is even now the most important element of Indian religions."[4]

This "most important element of Indian religions" in its major text has finally begun to attract a scholarly attention commensurate with its importance. In the nineteenth century E. Burnouf[5] and H. H. Wilson[6] studied it. In this century S. Dasgupta[7] culled its philosophical import. E. Pargiter[8] analyzed it as a source for historical data. In the United States T. Hopkins[9] examined the *Bhāgavata* for its social teaching and Larry Shinn[10] reviewed its teaching about the relation of deity and *saṃsāra*. S. Bhaṭṭācārya[11] has presented a study of its metaphysics impressively, but with a dubious methodology. A. Sarma Biswas[12]

4. Surendranath Dasgupta, *A History of Indian Philosophy*, III (Cambridge : At the University Press, 1940), vii.

5. *Le Bhâgavata Purâna*; *ou, Histoire poetique de Krichna*. 5 vols. Vols. 1-3 translated and published by Eugène Burnouf (Paris : Imprimerie Royale, 1840-1847). Vol. 4 translated by M. Hauvette-Besnault (Paris : Imprimerie Nationale, 1884). Vol. 5 translated by A. Roussel (Paris : Imprimerie Nationale, 1898).

6. H. H. Wilson, *Essays Analytical, Critical and Philological* (London : Trubner & Co., 1864-1865).

7. Dasgupta, *A History of Indian Philosophy*.

8. F. E. Pargiter, *Ancient Indian Historical Tradition* (London : Oxford University Press, 1922) and *The Purāṇa Text of the Dynasties of the Kali Age* (London : Oxford University Press, 1913).

9. Thomas J. Hopkins, "The Vaishṇava Bhakti Movement in the *Bhāgavata Purāṇa*" (unpublished Ph.D. dissertation, Yale University 1961).

10. Larry Dwight Shinn, "Kṛṣṇa's *Līlā* : An Analysis of the Relationship of the Notion of Deity and the Concept of *Saṃsāra* in the *Bhāgavata Purāṇa* (unpublished Ph.D. dissertation, Princeton University, 1972).

11. Siddheśvara Bhaṭṭācārya, *The Philosophy of the Śrīmad-Bhāgavata* (2 vols.; Ranjit Ray, 1960-1962).

12. A. S. Sarma Biswas, *Bhāgavata Purāṇa: A Linguistic Study* (Dibrugarh : Vishveshvarand Book Agency, 1965).

has studied it linguistically and T. S. Rukmani[13] has given a survey of its general facets. Apart from the sectarian commentators, no one apparently has attempted an examination of the *Bhāgavata*'s religious structure.

From one point of view this has already been done by the earlier Indian scholars in such commentaries as Śrīdhara's or the sectarians', but these reflect their own sectarian milieus, differ among themselves, and are separated from the *Bhāgavata* by centuries. Undoubtedly the *Bhāgavata* had the dynamic potential for these developments, and a thorough study of the *Bhāgavata*'s theology should show this potential as well as show the sources from which it derived.[14] In this study we seek to make a beginning by examining the *Bhāgavata* in order to understand its religious structure, both implicit as well as explicit, through what may be called a 'redaction criticism.'

Unity and Date

Such a redaction criticism assumes a unitary authorship or composition. This is subject to question. In its literary style the *Bhāgavata* uses the device of question and answer, which results in narrations within narrations. For example, Sūta relates what he heard from Śuka who heard it from Vyāsa, or Sūta relates Kṛṣṇa's conversation with Uddhava, and so on. Such a device may be open to both interpolation and repeated redaction. On this question of the *Bhāgavata*'s unity, a general conclusion is possible, though subject to qualification, and even dissent from some scholars.

According to M. Winternitz, the *Bhāgavata* "is the one *Purāṇa* which, more than any of the others, bears the stamp of a unified composition, and deserves to be appreciated as a literary production on account of its language, style and

13. T. S. Rukmani, *A Critical Study of the Bhāgavata Purāṇa*, The Chowkhamba Sanskrit Studies, Vol. LXXVII (Varanasi : Chowkhamba Sanskrit Series Office, 1970).

14. Cf. J. A. B. van Buitenen's statement : "...the future became the commentary on a basic text." in "On the Archaism of the *Bhāgavata Purāṇa*" in Milton Singer, *Krishna : Myths, Rites, and Attitudes*, p. 37.

metre."[15] Its style is unusual, being complicated and archaic; in syntax its sentences are nearer to English word order than is usual in Sanskrit and its related languages. According to J. A. B. van Buitenen, while Vedic archaism was notably absent in classical Sanskrit, the *Bhāgavata* is a notable exception, especially within the Purāṇic tradition from the second to the tenth century A.D. He considers it "a unique phenomenon...when Sanskrit letters were in fact on the decline, a text purporting to belong to the Purāṇic tradition consciously attempted to archaize its language."[16]

Yet according to S. Dasgupta, "the *Bhāgavata* is a collection of accretions from different hands at different times and not a systematic whole."[17] He thinks the contradictions within its various narrations are too conspicuous to maintain any unity beyond the most extrinsic. P. Śāstri discerns two, perhaps three, revisions within the text.[18] Although there is some evidence for this in the convention of narration within narration, the evidence for a final redactor, who wrote and compiled a single version is convincing. As C. V. Vaidya sums up:

> ...It appears to be the work of one author. The diction is the same throughout; the manner of running longer Vṛttas is the same and the exposition or theory is the same. There may be some interpolations but they are few and far between, unlike those in the other Purāṇas. Indeed there are supposed to be 332 Adhyāyas in the Bhāgavata as stated in the Padma Purāṇa, and Śrīdhara has commented on 335 only. These three additional chapters are also pointed out. Hence it may be stated that the present Bhāgavata is the least tampered with Purāṇa we have and thus there is no difficulty in relying upon arguments drawn from an internal study of the Purāṇa as in other Purāṇas; for with regard

15. Moriz Winternitz, *A History of Indian Literature*, translated by S. Ketkar (New York: Russell & Russell, 1971), I, 556.

16. van Buitenen, "On the Archaism of the *Bhāgavata Purāṇa*," p. 24.

17. Surendranath Dasgupta, *A History of Indian Philosophy*, IV (Cambridge : At the University Press, 1949), 26.

18. P. Śāstri, "The Mahāpurāṇas," *Journal of the Bihar and Orissa Research Society*, XIV (1928), Part III, 323-40.

to the latter one is never certain, when relying upon any extract from them, as to whether these extracts do belong to the original Purāṇa or whether they are interpolations.[19]

For a study of the *Bhāgavata*'s religious structure, in addition to confidence in the text's unity, a knowledge of its place of origin and date, as clearly as these can be ascertained, is important. This information can only be derived circumstantially. Early European scholars, such as Colebrooke, Burnouf, and Wilson, thought that the *Purāṇa* was composed by the grammarian Vopadeva (ca. 1350), the author of an index to the *Bhāgavata*, the *Harilīlā*, but the theory is untenable. The terminus ad quem must be the catalogue of the *Purāṇas* in Alberuni's history (1030 A.D.). Since it gives greater detail to Kṛṣṇa's biography than either the *Harivaṃśa* or the *Viṣṇu Purāṇa*, the *Bhāgavata* probably postdates these texts of the third or fourth centuries.[20] Thus the limits for its dating are 500-1000 A.D. Within these limits opinion varies. From the references within the *Bhāgavata* apparently to the Vaiṣṇava Āḷvārs it appears that the *Bhāgavata* was written in South India, probably in a Tamil speaking area. For example: "There will be many in the Dravidian lands, where the rivers Tāmraparṇī, Kṛtamālā, Payasvinī, the most sacred Kāverī, Pratīcī and Mahānadī flow; those who drink their waters generally become pureminded devotees of Bhagavān Vāsudeva."[21] The main period of the Āḷvārs' activity can be placed in the eighth and ninth centuries. The *Bhāgavata*'s redactor may be considered the contemporary of these saints. Thus T. Hopkins' assessment seems correct: "The ninth century, probably between 850 and 900 A.D., would thus seem the most likely time for the *Bhāgavata* to have been written."[22] This, however,

19. C. V. Vaidya, "The Date of the *Bhāgavata Purāṇa*," *Journal of the Bombay Branch of the Royal Asiatic Society, New Series*, I (1925), 145-46.

20. Witernitz, *A History of Indian Literature*, I, 555.

21. XI. 5. 39-40: kvacitkvacinmahārāja draviḍeṣu ca bhūriśaḥ/ tāmraparṇī nadī yatra kṛtamālā payasvinī// kāverī/ ca mahāpuṇyā pratīcī ca mahānadī ye pibanti jalaṃ tāsāṃ manujā manujeśvara prāyo bhaktā bhagavati vāsudeve'malāśayāḥ// Cf. IV. 28. 30.

22. Hopkins, "Vaishṇava Bhakati Movement in the Bhāgavata *Purāṇa*," p. 7.

is a tentative assignment. With van Buitenen, we agree that until "fresh evidence turns up, it is better not to push back the date of the final version of the *Bhāgavata* too far, nor too uncompromisingly to insist on the southern origin of our text."[23] There are no references to the *Bhāgavata* in Rāmānuja (12th century) nor in Yāmuna (918-1038), both South Indian devotional theologians. "Their reticence", according to van Buitenen, "needs to be explained...That neither appears to quote from our text may mean either that in their day it was not sufficiently known or that it was not sufficiently respectable for their orthodox purposes. But argumentum e silentio are never conclusive...[24] Nevertheless, a reasonable working hypothesis dates the *Bhāgavata* around 900 A.D., and there seems to be no alternative to a South Indian origin.[25]

Authorship and Provenance

The *Bhāgavata* itself attributes its authorship to Vyāsa, the legendary compiler of the *Vedas* and the author of the *Mahābhārata* and of the *Brahma Sūtras*. In a charming conversation the sage Nārada tells Vyāsa that his inquiries were complete, that he had produced the *Mahābhārata*: "Have you not thoroughly comprehended whatever you desired to know, as you have compiled the great, wonderful *Bhārata* which is full of matters pertaining to the principal goals of human life ? The eternal Brahman which has been so much coveted by you has been known and attained by you. Still, O learned sage, you are worrying yourself as if you have not achieved your goal."[26] But Vyāsa asks Nārada to "explain to me sufficiently clearly the deficiency in me though I have dived deeply into the Supreme Brahman by Yogic practices and have mastered the *Vedas* by

23. van Buitenen, "On the Archaism of the *Bhāgavata Purāṇa*," p. 26.
24. Ibid.
25. F. Hardy confirms this assessment by showing that some passages of the *Bhāgavata* are translation-paraphrases of Āḷvār poems. See *Viraha Bhakti : The Early History of Kṛṣṇa Devotion in South India* (Delhi : Oxford University Press, 1983), p. 511-526.
26. I.5.3-4 : jijñāsitaṃ susaṃpannamapi te mahadadbhutam/kṛtavānbhārataṃ yastvaṃ sarvārthaparibṛṃhitam//jijñāsiṭamadhītaṃ ca brahma yattatsanātanam/ athāpi śocasyātmānamakṛtārtha iva prabho//

religious observances."[27] Nārada then chides Vyāsa: "You have not practically described the pure glory of Bhagavān. I think that knowledge...is incomplete...You have not really described the glory of Vāsudeva." Nārada tells him to "recollect with concentrated mind the various acts of the Wide-Strider for liberation from all bondages."[28]

The identity of the redactor of the *Bhāgavata* is important for an accurate description of its religious structure. Yet usually the identity of the redactor is derived from an investigation of that structure. Thus arguments can often be circular. With the issue complicated in this manner, certain parameters of the question may be discussed and some tentative conclusions reached. It has already been seen that Yāmuna and Rāmānuja of the Śrī-Vaiṣṇavas ignore or are unaware of the *Bhāgavata*. It would seem then that several schools or tendencies coexisted within what may broadly be called Bhāgavatism during the eighth through the eleventh centuries in South India. Besides the group which produced the *Bhāgavata* there were at least the following groups pertinent to this discussion: (1) the Āḷvārs who had a mystical devotion to the *avatāra* Kṛṣṇa uncomplicated by theological or philosophical theories; (2) the Pāñcarātras who were influenced by Tantrism and who had a developed theory of manifestations (*vyūha*) with little emphasis on the *avatāra* Kṛṣṇa; (3) the Śrī-Vaiṣṇavas who claimed for their camp both the Āḷvārs and the Pāñcarātras while modifying them in their own way. The Śrī-Vaiṣṇavas downplay the Kṛṣṇa of the Āḷvārs while they accept the Āḷvārs' emphasis on devotion and combine this with Pāñcarātra ritual. This group also considered the *Brahma Sūtras*, as interpreted by theistic commentators like Bodhāyana, authoritative. Over againt the Śrī-Vaiṣṇavas were the Bhāgavatas who produced the *Bhāgavata Purāṇa*. They too accepted the Āḷvārs, but with an emphasis on both devotion

27. I.5.7b: parāvare brahmaṇi dharmato vrataiḥ snātasya me nyūnamal aṃ vicakṣva//

28. I.5.8-9, 13 : bhavatā'nuditaprāyaṃ yaśo bhagavato'malam/ yenaivāsau na tuṣyeta manye taddarśanaṃ khilam// yathā dharmādayaścārthā munivaryānukīrtitāḥ/ na tathā vāsudevasya mahimā hyanuvarṇitaḥ//...atho mahābhāga bhavānamoghadṛk śuciśravāḥ satyarato dhṛtavrataḥ/urukramasyākhilabandhamuktaye samādhinānusmara tadviceṣṭitam//

and Kṛṣṇa, while they downplayed the Pāñcarātra rituals and theories. The following diagram shows the relationships.

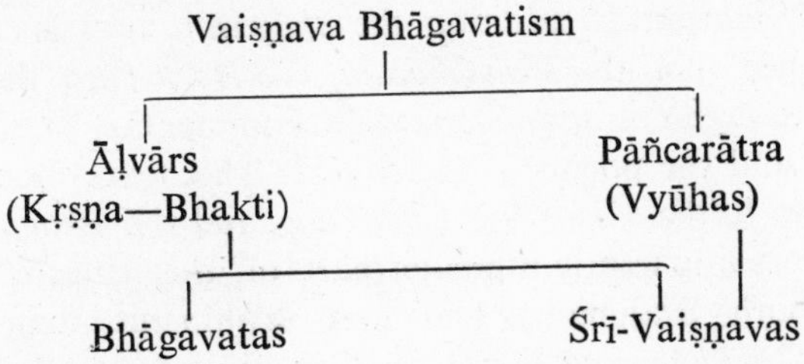

The question of Brahmanic orthodoxy or orthopraxis also is relevant to the question of the provenance of the *Bhāgavata*. T. Hopkins in an analysis of the *Bhāgavata*'s social teaching has observed that the *Bhāgavata* is relatively open on the issue of caste in contrast to the rigidity of the *dharma śāstras*. Devotion was open to *śūdras*, outcastes, and women. The exclusivist Brahmanic rites and disciplines are condemned. But because of the *Bhāgavata*'s consistent awareness of the Sanskrit literary tradition, Hopkins concludes :

> ...the actual writing of the *Bhāgavata* was probably done by scholarly ascetics who were opposed to the orthodox socio-religious system and to the abuses derived from it. They formed the leadership of the devotional movement, practicing and teaching bhakti based on faith and simplicity and free of the restrictions of orthodox religion. These exemplary devotees appealed to those who were poor and distressed through the misfortunes of birth and the inequities of the established order. The latter made up the mass support for the movement, which at the time of the *Bhāgavata* was an informal association of people drawn together by their common commitment to devotion. The views of both groups are evident in the *Bhāgavata* which presents an unequaled record of Vaishṇava devotionalism in its formative stages.[29]

29. Hopkins, "The Vaishṇava Bhakti Movement in the *Bhāgavata Purāṇa*," summary in the introductory material.

This interpretation seems to be too sociological. Although it brings to the fore literary evidence of an anti-Brahmanism, it does not account for the highly developed theological emphases of the *Bhāgavata*. In addition the *Bhāgavata* reveals a literary dependence upon the *Mahābhārata*, the *Harivaṁśa* the *Brahma Sūtras* (though not upon Śaṃkara's commentary[30]), the *Viṣṇu Purāṇa*, and the poems of the Āḷvārs. The text abounds with references to the *Vedas* the *Upaniṣads*, and the *Bhagavad Gītā*. These were apparently a greater part of the culture of South India, both Brahmanic, and non Brahmanic, than Hopkins allows. The *Bhāgavata* is not peculiar or exceptional in its social teaching; other texts were equally anti-Brahmanic.

J. A. B. van Buitenen points out that in "the labors of a Nāthamuni, a Yāmuna, a Rāmānuja, we observe a consistent effort to promote the Sanskritization of the *bhakti* religion."[31] In a similar way the author of the *Bhāgavata*, roughly contemporaneous with Nāthamuni, was concerned to legitimize the text. Its first verse contains a reference to both the *Brahma Sūtras* and to the Gāyatrī of the twice born.[32] Its use of language is often un-Pāṇinian; it consistently presents an archaic Vedic flavor. Thus van Buitenen asks: "Why did the author or authors responsible for the final version of the *Bhāgavata* want the book to sound Vedic ?"[33] His answer shows a very different provenance for the *Bhāgavata* than does Hopkins:' "we have a conspicuous concern to persuade others, if not oneself, of one's orthodoxy, because it is based on the Veda...The *Bhāgavata*'s point is: 'I am not only orthodox in the Vedic tradition, I even sound like

30. R. C. Hasra believes that Śaṃkara knew of the *Bhāgavata Purāṇa*, although this is extremely doubtful, see *New Indian Antiquary*, I (November (1938), 522-28. Others, i.e., K. A. Nilakantha Sastri in *A History of South India* (London : Oxford University Press, 1958), p. 332, and C. V. Vaidya in "The Date of the *Bhāgavata Purāṇa*," *Journal of the Bombay Branch of the Royal Asiatic Society*, New Series, I (1925), 148-53, assert that the *Bhāgavata* knew and reacted to Śaṃkara's teaching. This too is doubtful as we shall show.

31. van Buitenen, "On the Archaism of the *Bhāgavata Purāṇa*," p. 33.

32. I.1.1. refers to the *Brahma Sutras* I.1.2 : janmādyasya yataḥ/

33. van Buitenen, "On the Archaism of the *Bhāgavata Purāṇa*," p. 24.

the Veda."[34] Further in South India with its comparatively recent intermixture of Aryan with Tamil influences, the *Bhāgavata* movement with its devotion to the divine child Kṛṣṇa was especially suspect among circles whose court of appeal was the most ancient Aryan Sanskrit texts and customs. "Writing in Sanskrit," according to van Buitenen, "was not enough; to the faithful the supremacy of Krishnaism was hardly in doubt, but the high-sounding language (which often must have been unintelligible) gave appropriate notice of its Vedic orthodoxy."[35]

W. G. Archer proposes a further nuance to the discussion about the orientation of the *Bhāgavata*'s redactor. Of the two strands of the Kṛṣṇa legend, Kṛṣṇa as warrior prince and Kṛṣṇa as romantic cowherder lover, the warrior prince had been accommodated into the mainstream of the emergent Hindu tradition considerably earlier than the romantic lover. At the time of the *Bhāgavata* the romantic motif was still suspect, and was to remain suspect in some circles for centuries to come. The Kṛṣṇa of the *Bhagavad Gītā* and of the *Mahābhārata* was canonized in the tradition by the second century A.D. Rāmānuja in the twelfth century and Madhva in the thirteenth century downplayed the romantic lover element in Kṛṣṇa's biography. Thus Archer hypothesizes that within the *Bhāgavata* the editors, though including the scandalous episodes of Kṛṣṇa's romances, were biased toward Kṛṣṇa's heroic exploits. As he says: "But there can be little doubt that its Brahman authors were in the main more favourably inclined towards the hero prince than towards the cowherd lover."[36] This opinion is somewhat surprising, or perhaps ironic, since those *ācāryas* who most valued the *Bhāgavata*, Vallabha and Caitanya, based their teaching and devotion almost solely on Kṛṣṇa as romantic lover.

Each of these three views illustrates the difficulty in situating the *Bhāgavata*. Hopkins correctly ascertains a strong heterodox teaching about Brahmanic religious practice. He is incorrect, however, in attributing this heterodoxy to the final redactor.

34. *Ibid.*, p. 31.
35. *Ibid.*, p. 38.
36. W. G. Archer, *The Loves of Krishna in Indian Painting and Poetry* (London : George Allen and Unwin, 1957), p. 71.

Following van Buitenen's linguistic evidence it seems that the final redactor was attempting to legitimize his devotion to Kṛṣṇa by accenting the *Bhāgavata*'s Vedic qualities. Archer misjudges the situation. It is true that scandal was taken in certain circles at the stories of Kṛṣṇa's romances, for instance, among the Śrī-Vaiṣṇavas, but the redactor of the *Bhāgavata* wrote the last of the *Mahāpurāṇas,* not the first of the Vaiṣṇava commentaries on the *Brahma Sūtras*. The genre itself encouraged inclusiveness and extravagance; the overwhelming preponderance of the tenth canto within the *Bhāgavata* highlights rather than downplays Kṛṣṇa as romantic lover.

As a starting point for a study of the *Bhāgavata*'s theological and religious structure, the data of scholarship up to this time indicates that the actual writing of the *Bhāgavata* was done within a group of learned ascetics, probably Brahmans, in the South who, while remaining steadfast to their tradition of devotion to Kṛṣṇa, were attempting to legitimize that devotion within the broader Hindu tradition of the North. Their choice of the Purāṇic genre indicates that the narration of Kṛṣṇa's life story was important to them while at the same time the genre enabled them to collate their complex traditions. It also indicates that their teaching had not yet reached the stage where a systematics was possible, for example in a commentary on the *Brahma Sūtras.* They had been heavily influenced by the Āḷvārs, but not as much by the Pāñcarātras nor by the Śrī-Vaiṣṇavas—if that school had indeed reached any identity at that time.

Purāṇic Genre

At this point a discussion of the Purāṇic genre would be helpful. Traditionally the Purāṇa is defined as *pañcalakṣaṇa,* having five characteristics. Thus the *Matsya Purāṇa* gives the five characteristics as : (1) creation, (2) re-creation, (3) geneology of the gods, (4) the Manu-periods of time, and (5) histories of dynasties.[37] Of the extant *Purāṇas,* perhaps only the *Viṣṇu Purāṇa*

37. *Matsya Purāṇa* : sargaśca pratisargaśca vaṃśo manvantarāṇi ca/ vaṃśānucaritan caiva purāṇaṃ pañcalakṣaṇam// Cf. II.10.1 : atra sargo visargaśca sthānaṃ poṣaṇamūtayaḥ/ manvantareśānukathā nirodho muktirāśrayaḥ//

conforms fully to this definition, although as topics each of the five characteristics is found within the *Purāṇas*. According to A. D. Pusalker, "*Pañcalakṣaṇa* occupies but an insignificant part (about 1/40) of the extant *Purāṇas*."[38] The *Bhāgavata*, however, relying on the *Viṣṇu Purāṇa*, acknowledges the five characteristics,[39] but it then expands the definition to ten characteristics. The ten are (1) creation in general (*sarga*), (2) the creation by Brahmā (*visarga*), (3) maintenance of the creation (*sthāna*), (4) grace (*poṣaṇa*), (5) desire (*ūti*), (6) the Manu-periods of time (*manvantara*), (7) discourse on God (*īśānukathā*), (8) the cosmic dissolution (*nirodha*), (9) liberation (*mukti*), and (10) support or resort (*āśraya*).[40] The key addition is *āśraya* (or *apāśraya*), the support or Brahman toward which the other nine characteristics are aimed. "That from which creation and destruction are definitely known to emerge is the resort which is called the Supreme Brahman, the Supreme Self, etc."[41]

This expansion of the 'five characteristics' into 'ten characteristics' is pivoted on the tenth characteristic, Brahman (*āśraya*). It transforms the Purāṇic genre from one primarily interested in preserving ancient lore and legend into a genre capable of bearing the profoundest theological and religious import. At the same time the genre remains inclusive of that ancient lore and legend, which is now subordinated to a theological principle, Brahman. An investigation into the religious structure of the *Bhāgavata* must bear primarily on the meaning and import of that Brahman and will concern the other nine characteristics insofar as they illuminate the import of Brahman. Thus the question can now be posed about the ultimate religious structure of the *Bhāgavata*. In terms of a typological understanding of its teaching about Brahman, which of the three types of Hindu theology is it or does it tend to : *abheda* or identity (Śrīdhara), *bheda* or difference (Madhva), or *bhedābheda* or difference-in-identity (Vallabha and the Caitanya school) ? This question can

38. A. D. Pusalker, *Studies in Epics and Purāṇas of India* (Bombay : Bharatiya Vidya Bhavan, (1963), p. 23.

39. Cf. XII. 7. 10b.

40. II. 10.1 in note 37; cf. XII. 7.9-10.

41. II. 10.7: ābhāsaśca nirodhaśca yataścādhyavasīyate/sa āśrayaḥ paraṃ brahma paramātmeti śabyate//

be asked of the text both explicitly, that is, from its own teaching, and implicitly, that is, from its over-all import and meaning. The concern with its implicit religious structure is here more important because as a *Purāṇa* the *Bhāgavata* is largely a compilation whose explicit texts subserve the implicit theological import presumed by its unitary authorship or redaction.

Contents of the Bhāgavata

The *Bhāgavata* is a combination of discursive teaching and narratives about the manifestations of Bhagavān. The narratives of cantos four through ten are framed by the didactic discourses of cantos one through three and of cantos eleven and twelve. Ostensibly the *Purāṇa* was written by Vyāsa at Nārada's prompting. It was related with additional comment by Śuka, Vyāsa's son, to Sūta, who recited it for the sages at Naimiṣāraṇya.

In canto one Sūta tells the sages how Vyāsa came to compose the *Purāṇa*. There is a lengthy discourse on the merits of listening to the glorious activities of the Lord and an enumeration of the manifestations (*avatāra*) of Bhagavān. We hear the stories of Parīkṣit, Bhīṣma, and of Kṛṣṇa's disappearance from the world. The canto ends with Parīkṣit asking Sūta questions to which the following eleven cantos are the response.

Most of canto two is a discourse on a Sāṃkhya scheme of creation and an enumeration of Bhagavān's manifestations. The ten characteristics of a *Purāṇa* are mentioned in its final chapter.

The third canto is related by Maitreya to Vidura. Maitreya tells Vidura about the qualities of the Supreme Truth and the nature of the individual self. An important part of the third canto is Kapila's instructions to his mother Devahūtī concerning Sāṃkhya, Yoga, and devotion.

The fourth through ninth cantos contain many legends, typical of the Purāṇic genre, about Bhagavān's manifestations and ancient dynasties. There are historical references throughout this material. Many of the tenets of the discourses of the other cantos are illustrated in these stories. Prahlāda is described, for example, as a paradigmatic devotee.

The tenth canto is the longest since it describes in detail the life of Bhagavān Kṛṣṇa. It is divided into two parts. The first treats Kṛṣṇa's boyhood in Vṛndāvana and his erotic sports with the cowherd girls. The second describes how Kṛṣṇa overcame the tyrant Kaṃsa and his subsequent battles with Kālayavana, Jarāsandha, and Sālva. The *Mahābhārata* war is not treated in any detail in the *Bhāgavata*. Chapter eighty-seven discusses the problem of the transcendence and immanence of Bhagavān.

The eleventh canto again takes up the discourses left off in canto three. The characteristics of a devotee, of Sāṃkhya, and of the disciplines (*yoga*) of knowledge, action, and devotion are taught here.

The twelfth canto continues the royal histories of canto nine. Then Parīkṣit prepares for his death, and Śuka teaches him about Brahman and the Highest Truth. The origin of the *Vedas* is treated and the *Purāṇa* is concluded with a recapitulation of its contents. The *Bhāgavata* at the end is acclaimed as the greatest *Purāṇa*.

Method of Redaction Criticism

This study will therefore be a redaction criticism. It will seek to go beyond the questions of authorship, of the possible composite nature of the work, of the identity and extent of sources. Rather the theological meaning and religious structure of the whole, the finished product, is its main concern. Borrowing from contemporary Christian Biblical studies, this redaction criticism, in the words of Norman Perrin :

> ... is concerned with the interaction between an inherited tradition and a later interpretive point of view. Its goals are to understand why the items from the tradition were modified and connected as they were, to identify the theological motifs that were at work in composing a 'finished Gospel' [sc. *Purāṇa*], and to elucidate the theological point of view which is expressed in and through the composition.[42]

A redaction criticism of the *Bhāgavata* should show the genius of its Purāṇic genre in which an inherited tradition is brought to bear for its present purpose which is also pregnant with a

42. Norman Perrin, *What is Redaction Criticism* ? (Philadelphia : Fortress Press, 1969), pp. vi-vii.

future development. The *Purāṇa* is a mixture of historical reminiscence and legend, of interpreted tradition, of teachings borrowed for the purpose of corroboration and correlation, and, above all, of the free creativity of the author-redactor.

This type of criticism forms the framework for the study which follows. Non-dualism is at the heart of the *Bhāgavata*'s vision of God. This non-dualism is qualified by a Sāṃkhya assertion that the evolution of the universe is from a single principle. Devotion to Kṛṣṇa provides a driving force for the vigor of this qualified non-dualism. Two varieties of devotion are contained in the *Bhāgavata* : one reenforces the transcendence and inclusivity of Bhagavān, the other strengthens the reality of the devotee as an immanent form of the transcendent Deity. The major interpretations of the later theologians of the *Bhāgavata* show how these trends could be developed by a theological tradition both in continuity and discontinuity with the original source.

Thus each of the major forces and sources which determine the religious structure of the *Bhāgavata* will be discussed. The *Bhāgavata* at its moment in the history of Hinduism captured in a creative interaction the ideals and ideas which were religiously motivating both the saints and the common man. With non-dualism in the background and devotion to Bhagavān Kṛṣṇa in the foreground, the *Bhāgavata* sought to inspire the listener and to show him the coherent grandeur of its vision of a majestic God who contained within himself all the works of creation, who condescended to play among his creatures, all the while existing in a timeless majesty unsullied by any taint of imperfection. The *Bhāgavata* is a literary masterpiece, although its genre is strange to Western taste, but more than that it is a religious document which is the dynamic force behind a long and glorious chapter in the religious history of the Indian people.

CHAPTER II

THE NON-DUALISM OF THE *BHĀGAVATA*

The Supreme Person

An investigation of the teaching of the *Bhāgavata* about non-dualism (*advaita*) is complicated by several factors, not the least of which is the nature of the Purāṇic genre, which by its inclusiveness introduces differing names and terms for the Absolute, each with its own connotations. The *Bhāgavata* usually relies on the variegated Vedāntic vocabulary, but in addition it often uses a Sāṃkhya terminology. There is no doubt of the *Bhāgavata*'s non-dualist emphasis, yet its precise import and meaning are not immediately clear. S. Dasgupta, perhaps too hastily, remarks that as "regards the position of God and His relation to the world the outlook of the *Bhāgavata-Purāṇa* is rather ambiguous."[1] Non-dualism is prescribed differently of different subjects: Brahman, Ātman, Bhagavān, Puruṣa, etc. Is the difference terminological? Yet through this ambiguity it is possible to perceive a single import. The *Bhāgavata* itself states that it was written "for arriving at the accurate and real knowledge of the tenth charateristic," that is, *āśraya*.[2] *Āśraya* means "that...on which anything depends or rests," "the person or thing in which any quality...is inherent,"[3] an asylum, refuge, source, or origin. In this context *āśraya* is thus a synonym for Brahman or Bhagavān: "That from which creation and destruction are definitely known to emerge, is the

1. Dasgupta, *A History of Indian Philosophy*, IV, 18.
2. II. 10. 2a : daśamasya viśuddhyarthaṃ...lakṣaṇam/
3. Monier Monier-Williams, *A Sanskrit-English Dictionary* (Oxford : At the Clarendon Press, 1899), p. 158.

resort which is called the Highest Brahman, the Highest Self."[4] In another place Nārada advises Vyāsa to "recollect with concentrated mind the various acts of the Lord with wide steps for liberation from all bondages."[5] "Lord with wide steps" is an epithet of Vāmana, an avatāra of Viṣṇu, by extension of Kṛṣṇa, who is the Supreme Deity, the 'support' (*āśraya*), to which all else in the narrative is subordinated. Hence an examination of passages about non-dualism will show that there is a complex, sometimes obscure, teaching that Brahman, Ātman, Puruṣa, Bhagavān, etc. are non-dual. The question naturally arises: if the same quality is ascribed to these different subjects, are they identical? If not, is there a consistent sense or pattern in the ascription? Further, what ramifications does the perception, or deduction, of non-duality have for the apparent duality of God and the world, of individual self and the Highest Self?

The *Bhāgavata* in several passages indicates that non-dualism means that there is only one real existent. In the course of a lengthy discourse by Brahmā, who is the first created being derived from the Supreme Being, to Nārada, Brahmā sums up his insight into Bhagavan: "In this way, child, Bhagavān, the creator of all, has been described to you in brief. Whatever is sat or asat is not different from Hari."[6]

In a context describing the creation of the world and the various manifestations of God within it, Brahmā affirms Hari's all-pervading singleness: outside of him there is nothing. If there is anything its reality must be derived or exist within the greater reality of Hari. Again in an address to Brahmā, at the beginning of creation, when only Brahmā had as yet been created, Viṣṇu told him: "In the beginning, before the creation, I alone was in existence. There was nothing else—neither sat or asat nor their cause. After the creation of the universe what exists, is I. I am the universe. What remains is me."[7] In this context Viṣṇu's

4. II.10.7 : ābhāsaśca nirodhaśca yataścādhyavasīyate/sa āśrayaḥ paraṃ brahma paramātmeti śabdyate//

5. I.5.13b: urukramasyākhilabandhamuktaye samādhinānusmara tadviceṣṭitam//

6. II.7.50 : so'yaṃ te'bhihitastāta bhagavānviśvabhāvanaḥ/ samāsena harernānyadanyasmātsadasacca yat//

7. II.9.32 : ahamevāsamevāgre nānyadyatsadasatparam/paścādahaṃ yadetacca yo'vaśiṣyeta so'smyaham//

existence is placed within a temporal sequence of sole existence, creation, maintenance, destruction, and then sole existence again. This special message, which is secret, was passed on to Brahmā's son, Nārada, and thence to Vyāsa, the author of the *Bhāgavata*.

In the third canto the sequence of creation is described within a discussion between Vidura and Maitreya. Brahmā, after a hundred years of intense meditation, addresses Bhagavān Viṣṇu: "Bhagavān, after a very long time you have been realized by me today. It is indeed the defect of beings conditioned by body that your essential nature is not realized by them. Nothing other than you exists. Anything else is not pure because it is you who appear to be many due to the mixture of the qualities by your creative energy."[8] Here there is a sense of the simultaneity of Viṣṇu, of his first created, Brahmā, and also of the embodied beings who are yet to be created. Again creation is identified with the sole existent: "you who appear to be many." The cause of plurality is Bhagavān's creative energy (*māyā*) which introduces it into the sole existent. Ignorance of Bhagavān's non-duality is the disgrace of the embodied beings who have ignorance even though they are not yet manifest, still being in a subtle state. Nevertheless, even their ignorance does not sully Bhagavān's purity of existence.

In canto six Janārdana (Kṛṣṇa) revealed his form as the Supreme Person to the subordinate creator, Dakṣa : "O Brahman, contemplation is my heart, worship is my body, activity is my form, sacrifices well-performed are the members of my body, the merit resulting from such sacrifices is my mind, and the gods are my vital airs." Here the only existent Self is described in moral terms. Before the creation he was the only existent in a state of inactivity : "In the beginning, I alone existed. There was nothing else as internal or external. I was pure consciousness and unmanifested. There was deep sleep everywhere."[9] The one

8. III.9.1 : jñāto'si me'dya sucirānnanu dehabhājāṃ na jñāyate bhagavato gatirityavadyam/nānyattvadasti bhagavannapi tanna śuddhaṃ māyāguṇavyatikarādyadururvibhāsi//

9. VI.4.46-47 : tapo me hṛdayaṃ brahmaṃstanurvidyā kriyākṛtiḥ/ aṅgāni kratavo jātā dharma ātmāsavaḥ surāḥ// ahamevāsamevāgre nānyatkiṃcāntaraṃ bahiḥ/ saṃjñānamātramavyaktaṃ prasuptamiva viśvataḥ//

existent is a person, made up only of pure consciousness (*saṃjñāna*), who kept back in an unmanifest state his infinite possibilities in a deep sleep. The activities and religious duties of embodied beings go on in some unmanifested, transcendental state within this eternal Person. This non-dual Person has unbounded possibilities for plurality

After the death of Hiraṇyakaśipu at the hands of the Man-Lion in the seventh canto, Prahlāda addressed the Lord in his Man-Lion form: "You are air, fire, earth, sky, and water, the objects of the senses, the vital airs, the senses, heart, intellect and ego; everything possessed of qualities or devoid of qualities is you. There is nothing other than you even if conveyed by mind or speech, Lord."[10] This eulogy is addressed to the Man-Lion by a demon, an enemy of God, but the language is of one within the created world, who sees the Lord in the things before him, yet realizes his transcendent nature. The Supreme Person, who is the only one, appears in the world as the objects of the world, both material and psychic. Non-duality here takes on the aspect of inclusiveness. What is, is the Lord.

The One and the Many

Non-duality does not mean that the sole existent being cancels out plurality. The *Bhāgavata* has many passages in which non-duality is described as within the sphere of plural forms. In the seventh canto Nārada tells Yudhiṣṭhira that not only those who love Bhagavān attain him but also those who hate him. This follows from the fact that the non-dual dwells within every creature as its inner Self. Nārada says that Bhagavān is one without a second. How then can the Supreme be violent or chastise his foes? The answer is that the mind should be fixed on him who is not other than oneself, thus love and hatred both bring about the same result: "A mortal may not achieve such an absorption into him through the discipline of devotion as through constant enmity; this is my conclusion."[11] Liberation is grounded in non-

10. VII.9.48: tvaṃ vāyuragnirviyadambumātrāḥ prāṇendriyāṇi hṛdayaṃ cidanugrahaśca/sarvaṃ tvameva saguṇo viguṇaśca bhūmannānyattvadastyapi manovacasā niruktam//

11. VII.1.26: yathā vairānubandhena martyastanmayatāmiyāt/ na tathā bhaktiyogena iti me niścitā maitḥ//

duality, as well as plurality, which is a state of being unliberated. Fixed meditation on the Supreme Being, whether from love or hatred, brings about the realization of non-duality because he is the Self within all things.

This is further illustrated in canto three in a Sāṃkhya passage, which describes the non-duality of the one and the many as an appearance of being in non-being : "The sage attains the non-dual, which is distinct from the body, which appears as real in the unreal, which is friend to the real, which is the eye to the unreal, which is woven into everything."[12]

The non-dual existent is within all that is relatively non-existent in order to provide a basis for liberation. The non-dual appears in the non-existent and because it is its appearance it is bound to it. Though non-dual, it is 'woven' together with all that is many. Thus the many is only relatively non-existent.

Identity is described in the *Bhāgavata* as non-difference (*abheda*). Usually non-difference refers to the relation of cause and effect. Those who really know Kṛṣṇa see everything as a manifestation of him. There is nothing other than him because "of all things that exist their essence lies in their cause. Bhagavān Kṛṣṇa is the cause of all these causes. Hence, what cause can be affirmed apart from him ?"[13] If cause and effect are identical, then Kṛṣṇa, as cause of all that is, is identical with those effects. As cause of the various causes, Kṛṣṇa becomes the real essence of all effects. Texts like these recall the Sāṃkhya doctrine of *satkārya*, the inherent presence of the effect in the cause, though this text goes considerably beyond that doctrine by premising non-difference to the extent of not even talking of effects apart from Kṛṣṇa.

A similar text is Hiraṇyakaśipu's eulogy of Brahmā in canto three. This text is a little unusual for the *Bhāgavata* in that it treats Brahmā, who is the first created being and who in turn is the creator of all subsequent creation, as synonymous with the Supreme Deity. Brahmā, rather than being an autonomous creation, is considered as that aspect of the Deity which is

12. III.27.11 : muktaliṅgaṃ sadābhāsamasati pratipadyate/tato bandhumasaccakṣuḥ sarvānusyūtamadvayam//

13. X.14.57 : sarveṣāmapi vastūnāṃ bhāvārtho bhavati sthitaḥ/ tasyāpi bhagavānkṛṣṇaḥ kimatadvastu rūpyatām//

creative : "You are the immutable Self occupying the highest place, unborn, all-pervading, the supporter and controller of all living beings". As the Highest Self Brahmā pervades everything. The chain of causes can be traced back to him and thus nothing can be said to be totally distinct from him: "There is nothing apart from you, cause or effect, mobile or immobile; the sciences and their branches are your bodies, you are the golden womb of the universe, the great possessor of the three qualities."[14] In comparison to the passage previously quoted, this text makes allowance for a greater diversity within the non-difference of the Supreme Deity.

Nārada in his coversation with Yudhiṣṭhira demonstrates how a reflection on non-difference yields three different aspects of non-dualism :

> The sage shaking off the three dream states (waking, dreaming, dreamless sleeping) through understanding himself meditates on the non-duality of thought [*bhāvādvaitam*], the non-duality of action [*kriyādvaitam*], and the non-duality of substance [*dravyādvaitam*].
>
> Examining the substantial unity of cause and effect, as in the weaving of cloth from thread since their diversity is unreal —this is called the non-duality of thought.
>
> O Pārtha, resigning all of one's actions of mind, speech, and body, directly to the Highest Brahman—this is called the non-duality of action.
>
> Identifying one's own interests and desires with that of one's wife, children, etc. and of all other embodied beings—this is called non-duality of substance.[15]

14. VII.3.31b-32 *:* kūṭastha ātmā parameṣṭhyajo mahāṃstvaṃ jivalokasya ca jīva ātmā// tvattaḥ paraṃ nāparamapyanejadejacca kiṃcidvyatiriktamasti/ vidyākalāste tanavaśca sarvā hiraṇyagarbho' si bṛhattripṛṣṭaḥ//

15. VII.15.62-64 : bhāvādvaitaṃ kriyādvaitaṃ dravyādvaitaṃ tathātmanaḥ/ vartayansvānubhūtyeha trīnsvapnāndhunute muniḥ// kāryakāraṇavastvaikyamarśanaṃ paṭatantuvat/ avastutvādvikalpasya bhāvādvaitaṃ taducyate// yadbrahmaṇi pare sākṣātsarvakarmasamarpaṇam/ manovāktanubhiḥ pārtha kriyādvaitaṃ taducyate// ātmajāyāsutādināmanyeṣāṃ sarvadehinām / yatsvārthakāmayoraikyaṃ dravyādvaitaṃ taducyate//

Here in this marvelous summary of Vedāntic teaching, the *Bhāgavata* grounds its teaching concerning different kinds of actions (*pravṛtta* and *nivṛtta*) in an ever-deepening insight into non-duality. The surrender of the fruits of one's actions is called *kriyādvaita* or, as S. Bhaṭṭācarya says, "the spiritual act that discards the duality of *pravṛtta* and *nivṛtta* actions [injunctions and prohibitions]." When this has been achieved, the non-duality of substance becomes possible, "an all-embracing altruism which breaks through the dichotomy between 'I' and 'mine' on the one hand and the rest of the world on the other."[16] These two modes of non-duality are ultimately resolved in the non-duality of thought in which the dichotomy between the single Cause and the world of plurality is dissolved in a vision of non-differenced unity.

But what is this non-differenced, non-dual reality ? In certain passages the *Bhāgavata* says that it is knowledge or consciousness itself. Thus in the first canto where the program for the *Bhāgavata* is being laid out, Sūta replies to the questions of the sages by pointing out that "the aim of life is inquiry into the Truth and not (the desire for enjoyment in heaven) by performing religious rites. Those who possess the knowledge of the Truth call the knowledge of non-duality as the Truth; it is called Brahman, the Highest Self, and Bhagavān."[17] The non-duality of Truth or the reality (*tattva*) is such that no ultimate distinction between knower and knowledge can be made, though by giving the absolute reality different names, the *Bhāgavata* affirms that the richness of absolute reality cannot be exhausted by considering it from one angle only. With admitting any distinction within the absolute reality, the *Bhāgavata* draws on various traditions to aid the understanding. The terms 'Brahman' and 'Highest Self' are drawn from the Vedānta, while 'Bhagavān' is dear to the Vaiṣṇavas. The final position given to Bhagavān seems to raise it above the other two in importance, and this is borne out by the *Purāṇa* as a whole. Thus non-dual knowledge,

16. Bhaṭṭācarya, *The Philosophy of the Śrīmad-Bhāgavata*, I, 267-68.

17. I.2.10b-11: jīvasya tattvajijñāsā nārtho yaśceha karmabhiḥ// vadanti tattattvavidastattvaṃ yajjñānamadvayam/brahmeti paramātmeti bhagavāniti śabdyate//

which is the essence of the absolute reality, is, according to the *Bhāgavata*, ultimately personal.

Again, when Brahmā recites the primordial *Bhāgavata* in the second canto to Nārada, he asserts that the Puruṣa's "real nature is absolute, real knowledge which is pure, underlying the interior of all, accurate, changeless and qualityless. Being the Truth, it is perfect, full, beginningless and endless, eternal and non-dual."[18]

The personal nature of absolute reality and its non-duality are affirmed along with its identity with absolute knowledge (*kevalaṃ jñānam*) In the tenth canto Rukmiṇī tells her husband Kṛṣṇa that it is true that "you abide in the ocean (of the heart) as if afraid of the three qualities, being the Supreme Self of infinite pure consciousness."[19]

The absolute reality is consciousness (*upalambhana*) and he resides in the heart of the devotee. He is a person, specifically Kṛṣṇa, who is identified with the Wide-Strider, Viṣṇu.

The Absolute 'With' and 'Without' Qualities

The last two passages quoted refer to the non-dual as 'qualityless' and 'afraid of qualities'. There are any number of passages in the *Bhāgavata* in which non-dualism is coupled with terms such as *nirguṇa*, *aguṇa*, *arūpa*, etc. The question arises whether these can be taken in the sense of Śaṃkara's *nirguṇa* Brahman. According to T. S. Rukmani, "the philosophic teaching of the *Bhāgavata Purāṇa* stands nearer to Śaṃkara's system than to the theistic Sāṃkhya which dominates the other Purāṇic works."[20] However, an examination of passages which use these terms will reveal that they have a different import than Śaṃkara's *nirguṇa* Brahman.

The above-mentioned texts[21] where Puruṣa and Ātman are described as 'qualityless,' *nirguṇa*, both occur in contexts in

18. II.6.39 : vaśuddhaṃ kevalaṃ jñānaṃ pratyaksamyagavasthitam/ satyaṃ pūrṇamanādyantaṃ nirguṇaṃ nityamadvayam//

19. X.60.35a: satyaṃ bhayādiva guṇebhya urukramāntaḥ śete samudra upalambhanamātra ātmā/

20. Rukmani, *A Critical Study of the Bhāgavata Purāṇa*, p. 4.

21. II.6.39 and X.60.35a.

which the Supreme Deity, whether as Puruṣa or as Kṛṣṇa, is engaged with a universe evolving from him. This association of what is without qualities with what has qualities is characteristic of the non-dualism of the *Bhāgavata*. A number of texts illustrate this point. For example, in canto one Sūta says that "this form of Bhagavān, who indeed has no form, consisting of consciousness, has been created in the Self through the qualities of his creative energy, the Great Principle, etc.[22] He who has no form is capable of assuming form for his own purposes. The lack of form is related to his essential nature as consciousness, which is untouched ultimately by his own work in creation. Further a Sāṃkhya-like scheme of creation-emanation is implied in the use of the concepts of 'creative energy' (*māyā*) and the 'Great Principle' (*mahat*). The qualities (*guṇa*) are the constituents, though noumenal, of the created universe, and by definition are not related to the essence of the Absolute. The qualities are used by the Absolute's creative energy: "Though he is qualityless, he, through his creative energy, has assumed the three qualities, namely, *sattva*, *rajas*, and *tamas*, for the maintenance, creation, and dissolution (of the universe)".[23] The universe is placed within Nārāyaṇa, who accepts the qualities for its creation.[24] In canto eight Brahmā when eulogizing Hari says that he is the infinite one: "you are without qualities, and yet are master of all qualities, and who are established in *sattva*.[25] In the latter passage Hari is beyond description and devoid of qualities. The lack of qualities puts him beyond his own creation and leaves him uncontaminated, yet master of those qualities. The lack of qualities does not mean that the absolute reality is nothing, rather that he is incomprehensible. Nor does it signify that the Supreme Deity lacks anything. This description of *nirguṇa* does not indicate that Puruṣa, Ātman, Hari, or Bhagavān, when so described are equal to Śaṃkara's *nirguṇa* Brahman since their

22. I.3.30 : etadrūpaṃ bhagavato hyarūpasya cidātmanaḥ/ māyāguṇair-viracitaṃ mahadādibhirātmani//

23. II.5.18 : sattvaṃ rajastama iti nirguṇasya guṇāstrayaḥ/ sthitisarga-nirodheṣu gṛhītā māyāya vibhoḥ//

24. Cf. II.6.30.

25. VIII.5.50b : nirguṇāya guṇeśāya sattvasthāya ca sāṃpratam//

relation to Brahman with qualities or to his creative energy is never described as based purely and simply on an essential ignorance (*avidyā*). The relation of the Absolute to the qualities or to the creative energy is usually described as that of possession, and there is nowhere a disclaimer that these statements are a concession to the individual's limited capacity to understand. The *Bhāgavata*'s own particular use of 'creative energy' (*māyā*) and ignorance (*avidyā*) will be examined in greater detail further on.

It is by no means insignificant that the opening verse of the *Bhāgavata* relates the absolute reality, Brahman, to creation. Here in what S. Dasgupta calls "probably the most important passage in the *Bhāgavata*,"[26] the highest truth is indissolubly linked to the phenomenal world of creation, which is described as 'not false' (*amṛṣā*):

> Him from whom is the creation, etc. of this (universe), inferred by positive and negative concomitance in things; all-knower, self-luminous; who revealed to the heart of the First Sage the Vedas; about whom the sages are confused; in whom the threefold evolution is real as is the transformation (exchange) of fire, water earth; by his own strength (in his own abode) always free from deception; the True, the Supreme, on Him we meditate.[27]

Though this verse has been interpreted to mean that creation through the three qualities is false, its most obvious sense is precisely the opposite. Since the Lord is self-luminous (*svarāṭ*) and free from deception, creation has reality from his reality. As Sūta tells the sages: "Just as one (same) fire permeates the pieces of wood from which it is created, so the Person, the Self of the universe, appears in different things."[28] As the source of everything that is, the Person permeates all things as their inner Self (*ātman*).

26. Dasgupta, *A History of Indian Philosophy*, IV, 33.

27. I.1.1 : janmādyasya yato'nvayāditarataścārtheṣvabhijñāḥ svarāṭ tene brahma hṛdā ya ādikavaye muhyanti yatsūrayaḥ/tejovārimṛdāṃ yathā vinimayo yatra trisargo' mṛṣā dhāmnā svena sadā nirastakuhakaṃ satyaṃ paraṃ dhīmahi//

28. I.2.32 : yathā hyavahito vahnirdāruṣvekaḥ svayoniṣu/ nāneva bhāti viśvātmā bhūteṣu ca tathā pumān//

The *Bhāgavata*'s non-dualism in these creation passages sometimes equates, while immediately qualifying that equation, the universe with Bhagavān, who is "indeed the universe, yet different from it; from him is the creation, destruction, and maintenance of the world."[29] In canto eight Śiva praised Hari for being "god of gods, pervader of the universe, the Lord of the universe, consisting of the universe. You are the Self, the cause and the controller of all things...The Brahman from which proceeds, the beginning, middle, and end of this (universe), but who being unchangeable is not affected by these; who constitutes this, the external thing as well as 'I', the other."[30] It is as if the *Bhāgavata* were searching for metaphors and concepts to describe its ineffable vision of the relation of the Absolute with the created world. Thus here there is a non-duality of Brahman, who is truth and consciousness, and that which is other, the universe and the individual self. Another apt metaphor occurs in canto eight when Hiraṇyakaśipu says that the visible universe is the body of the Lord by which he enjoys the qualities, mind, the vital airs and the senses, although "remaining all the while established in your original exalted state. You are the unmanifest Self and the most ancient Person."[31] The Lord as Self pervades the universe as a soul pervades the body. The body is part of, although distinct from, the whole person. Just so the world is part of, although distinct from, the totality which is Bhagavān.

One of the most celebrated incidents narrated in the *Bhāgavata* is in canto ten where Yaśodā reprimands the child Kṛṣṇa for eating dirt while at play. Kṛṣṇa says that he had not eaten dirt and opened his mouth to show his mother. Inside she saw the entire universe, the mountains, oceans, the heavens, stars, and lightning. She saw not only the material world, but also the psychic world, the senses, the mind, the objects of the senses, and the three qualities. "At the same time she saw in his

29. I.5.20a : idaṃ hi viśvaṃ bhagavānivetaro yato jagatsthāna-nirodhasaṃbhavāḥ/

30. VIII.12.4-5 : devadeva jagadvyāpin jagadīśa jaganmaya/ sarveṣāmapi bhāvānāṃ tvamātmā heturīśvaraḥ// ādyantāvasya yanmadhyamidamanyadahaṃ bahiḥ/yato 'vyayasya naitāni tatsatyaṃ brahma cidbhavān//

31. VII.3.33b : bhuñkṣe sthito dhāmani pārameṣṭhya avyakta ātmā puruṣaḥ purāṇaḥ//

wide open mouth the variegated universe, divided into individual selves, time, their inherent tendency and inherited destiny, the seed of action, along with Vraja and herself, and she was seized with terror." She realized that her son was the Lord. He then "cast the creative energy of Viṣṇu so that she again felt affection for her son."[32] She lost her knowledge of the Self and took her son on her lap. Such is the awesome lordship of Bhagavān, the awesome knowledge of the great mystery of Bhagavān's relation to the universe, that mere mortals may not bear to know of it casually.

Thus the *Bhāgavata* illustrates the ineffable non-duality of Kṛṣṇa, who is beyond the qualities, yet as their source, possesses them within himself. He is both *nirguṇa*, without qualities, and *saguṇa*, with qualities. This non-duality is usually just asserted and apparently contradictory statements are juxtaposed paradoxically. The mere mortal, such as Yaśodā, is stricken with terror at the immense mystery of the Lord's nature, which creates multiplicity within his own unity.

Non-dualism and the Self

The same mysterious non-duality grounds the relation of the Highest Self (*Paramātman*) and the individual self (*jīvātman*). The identity of the Highest Self and the individual self is the central teaching of the *Upaniṣads* and the Vedānta, where it is repeatedly stressed and explained by numerous examples and affirmed in countless texts. The *Bhāgavata* is clearly in this tradition: "That from which creation and destruction are definitely known to emerge is the resort which is called the Highest Brahman, the Highest Self."[33] In the third canto Maitreya tells Viṣṇu that he is one, the first of beings, the Self and the Lord of selves. "Truly, he was then this Seer and the only illuminator, he saw nothing." There was a time when he did not in-vision the universe. He thought that it was non-existent since his power

32. X.8.39,43b : etadvicitraṃ saha jīvakālasvabhāvakarmāśayaliṅgabhedam/ sūnostanau vīkṣya vidāritāsye vrajaṃ sahātmānamavāpa śaṅkām// ...vaiṣṇavīṃ vyatanonmāyāṃ putrasnehamayiṃ vibhuḥ//

33 II.10.7 : ābhāsaśca nirodhaśca yataścādhyavasīyate/ sa āśrayaḥ paraṃ brahma paramātmeti śabdyate//

was asleep, although deep within him his sight was intact: "That is truly the power of this Seer which is of the nature of both actual cause and potential effect. It is called the creative energy. It is by this power, that the all-pervading Lord created the universe."[34] This passage is pregnant with meaning. Bhagavān, the Self, was alone, although according to the Hindu cyclic understanding of time, which is inherent to God, his aloneness has been preceded by a time of creation, and that by a time of aloneness in an eternal pattern. By his own power the individual self did not exist phenomenally, but since this power has two phases, actual cause (*sat*)and potential effect (*asat*), the individual self in a certain sense eternally exists, whether manifest or unmanifest, within the Godhead. Bhagavān's power of vision continues even when his power is quiescent. The Self's power, his creative energy (*māyā*), brings forth both the material universe and the individual self. The Supreme Self is one, both when in a state of quiescence and when in a state of manifestation.

In the sixth canto Hari tells Citraketu that he is the Self, the creator of living beings. The Veda and Brahman are his forms. "One should understand that his own Self is pervading the whole of the universe and that the universe is resting on the Self and that both are pervaded by me." Just as a man who is asleep and dreams that the world is inside him, but when he wakes up he realizes that he is lying in a bed, so he should consider his waking states as the products of Bhagavān's creative energy. "Recognize me to be the Self or Brahman through which a person in a sleeping condition, regards himself as in a deep sleep. I am absolute bliss without qualities or senses."[35] The Self and Brahman are equivalent, both ground the manifest universe and the manifest selves. The universe as well as the individual self have a spiritual source and are ultimately

34. III.5.24a-25 : sa vā eṣa tadā draṣṭā nāpaśyaddṛśyamekarāṭ/...sā vā etasya saṃdraṣṭuḥ śaktiḥ sadasadātmikā/ māyā nāma mahābhāga yayedaṃ nirmame vibhuḥ//

35. VI.16.52,55 : loke vitatamātmānaṃ lokaṃ cātmani saṃtatam/ ubhayaṃ ca mayā vyāptaṃ mayi caivobhayaṃ kṛtam//...yena prasuptaḥ puruṣaḥ svāpaṃ vedātmanastadā/ sukhaṃ ca nirguṇaṃ brahma tamātmānamavehi mām//

the Self. Here the Upaniṣadic speculation on the continuity of the different states of waking, dreaming, etc. is recalled.

The non-duality of Self and individual self can be realized by the sages through a process of devotion based on knowledge and detachment. If they believe in that non-duality, they will find it within their own self.[36] This recognition of the Self within the individual self can be achieved by listening to the Veda. Thus the *Bhāgavata* emphasizes devotion with knowledge and detachment subordinated to it.

In canto four, after a long process of meditation and penance, the royal saint Malayadhvaja accepted Hari for his preceptor. He perceived the Self within his heart, "who is the witness of the mind." He saw that it was all pervading, in all things, and that all things were in it : "He realized himself as within the Highest Brahman and that the Highest Brahman was within himself. He then gave up even this consciousness and left the world."[37] Though manifested in and through the body, the Self is different from it. There are degrees of manifestation and because of this the individual self must pursue the highest Self where it is most manifest, in the interior of the individual self. Eventually it leaves off all manifestations and directs itself solely to its non-duality with the Highest Self. Knowledge of the Highest Self gives the devotee a sense of intimacy with him and accomplishes absorption into the Highest Self. Knowledge of the identity of the Self and the individual self removes the delusion that they are different in any ultimate sense.[38] Just as the Self diffused itself in the act of creation so it comes back to itself in the liberation of the individual self. Liberation is possible only because of the identity of the Highest Self and the individual self. It is a realization and return to a knowledge of what is real, leaving behind what is less real by means of a discipline of devotion combined with knowledge and detachment.

36. Cf. I.2.12.

37. IV.28.40,42 : sa vyāpakatayātmānaṃ vyatiriktatayātmani/ vidvān-svapna ivāmarśasākṣinaṃ virarāma ha//...pare brahmaṇi cātmānaṃ paraṃ brahma tathātmani/vīkṣamāṇo vihāyekṣāmasmāduparārāma ha//

38. Cf. I.9.42.

Bhagavān's Creative Energy

Lest, however, the teaching of the non-duality of the Highest Self and the individual self seem to completely nullify the reality of the created world, the *Bhāgavata* stresses in some passages a positive interpretation of non-dualism. In canto one Nārada tells Yudhiṣṭhira: "O King, this universe is the self-manifesting Bhagavān. He is one, the self of selves. He shines internally and externally. Look, he is manifold due to his creative energy."[39] This text, while affirming the non-duality of the created world and the Highest Self, interposes an intermediary force or power between the Self and the individual self and the world, namely, Bhagavān's creative energy (*māyā*). In many non-dualism texts, the creative energy is mentioned as a cause or motive for creation. It seems that the *Bhāgavata* uses this concept to explain the origin of the phenomenal selves and the phenomenal world, while maintaining their ultimate non-duality with the absolute reality, Bhagavān, who is unsullied by the act of creation. An examination of the *Bhāgavata*'s use of the concept '*māyā*' is also important because *māyā* is an important concept in the system of Śaṃkara.[40] If there is any dependence of the *Bhāgavata* upon Śaṃkara, or a related teaching, it should be revealed in its use of *māyā*.

In the third canto Vidura asks Maitreya: "O Brahman, how is it possible that qualities and activities can be predicated of Bhagavān, who is pure consciousness, without qualities and changeless, even by way of sport ?" In other words how could a transcendent Deity be associated with the phenomenal universe? "It is the desire in a child which propels it to play, and that desire comes from something else, but how for Bhagavān, who is self-satisfied and who is ever without a second. Bhagavān created the universe by his creative energy consisting of the qualities. It is by the creative energy that he sustains it and withdrews it. The Self is essentially knowledge and unaffected by

39. I.13.47 : tadidaṃ bhagavānrājanneka ātmātmanāṃ svadṛk/ antaro' nantaro bhāti paśya taṃ māyayorudhā//

40. Paul Hacker in "Relations of Early Advaitins to Vaisnavism," *Wiener Zeitschrift für die Kunde Süd-und Ost-asiens und Archiv fur indische Philosophie*, IV (1965), 147-48, suggests that Śaṃkara worked in a Vaiṣṇava milieu in which various forms of *advaita* were studied.

place, time, or condition either internally or externally. How can such a Self be united with the unborn (*māyā*) ?"[41] There is no doubt in Vidura's mind that *māyā* is the cause of the creation of the universe, but the Lord is of the nature of consciousness, is immovable, and without qualities. Can the two really be associated ? Śuka here interjects that they are incompatible and that their association is paradoxical: "It is the creative energy of Bhagavān, which is against all logic. Hence the affliction and bondage to (the soul who is essentially) free from bondage."[42] Because of this creative energy the individual self has the appearance of being bound, even though the bondage is unreal. The unreal, gets confused with the real, the less real with the ultimately real, and the dependent with the independent. The individual self in the world, founded on the creative energy of Bhagavān, is unreal, less real, or dependent, according to one's perspective. The Lord is ultimately real and independent. The source of the confusion is creative energy (*māyā*), which is the mediating principle of the *Bhāgavata* between the formless Lord and the formed universe, allowing and preserving the non-duality of Bhagavān and also the reality of the universe.[43]

The creative energy produces the three constituent qualities (*guṇa*), which are the noumenal starting point for the evolution of all phenomenal forms: "Though, without qualities, he, through his creative energy, has assumed the three qualities, being, activity, and inertia, for the maintenance, creation, and dissolution (of the universe)."[44]

A significant description of the creative energy is given in canto two when Bhagavān summarizes the *Bhāgavata* in four verses:

41. III.7.2-5 : brahmankathaṃ bhagavataścinmātrasyāvikāriṇaḥ/ līlayā cāpi yujyerannirguṇasya guṇāḥ kriyāḥ// krīḍāyāmudyamo'rbhasya kāmaścikrīḍiṣānyataḥ/ svatastṛptasya ca kathaṃ nivṛttasya sadā' nyataḥ// asrākṣīdbhagavānvisvaṃ guṇamayyātmamāyayā/ tayā saṃsthāpayatyetadbhūyaḥ pratyapidhāsyati// deśataḥ kālato yo'śāvavasthātaḥ śvato'nyataḥ/ aviluptāvabodhātmā sa yujyetājayā katham//

42. III.7.9 : seyaṃ bhagavato māyā yannayena virudhyate/ īśvarasya vimuktasya kārpanyamuta bandhanam//

43. Cf. I.3,30.

44. II.5.18 ; sattvaṃ rajastama iti nirguṇasya guṇāstrayaḥ/ sthitisarganirodheṣu gṛhītā māyayā vibhoḥ//

> In the beginning, before the creation, I alone was in existence. There was nothing else—neither the subtle nor the gross nor their cause. After the creation of the universe what exists is I. I am the universe. What remains is myself.
>
> That should be known as my creative energy on account of which there appears existence, despite its non-existence as independent reality, as in the case of false appearance, as in the case of the eclipsed planet Rahu.
>
> Just as the gross elements which may be said to have entered into created things, great or small, may be said not to have entered into them, similarly, I am in the elements as well as the creation from the elements, and also not in them.
>
> This much should be understood by him who desires to know the reality about the Self, the existence of which everywhere and at all times is inferred by positive and negative concomitance.[45]

Here the theory of the creative energy is tied into the doctrine of non-dualism. Through the entire process of creation, etc. Bhagavān is alone, yet because of the creative energy, a reflection or shadow makes its appearance. This appearance, in itself unreal, is real in its derivation from Bhagavān. He is in the appearance to the extent that it is real and not in it to the extent it is unreal. Verse thirty-three has been taken as a definition of the creative energy (*māyā*) : "That on account of which there appears existence, despite its non-existence as an independent reality."[46] Yet, out of context, this definition allows a greater unreality to the evolutes of the creative energy of Bhagavān than there should be for one who inquires into what exists at all times and in every place (*sarvatra* and *sarvadā*).

45. II.9.32-35 : ahamevāsamevāgre nānyadyatsadasatparam/ paścādahaṃ yadetacca yo'vaśiṣyeta so'smyaham// ṛte'rthaṃ yatpratīyeta na pratīyeta cātmani/ tadvidyādātmano māyāṃ yathābhāso yathā tamaḥ// yathā mahānti bhūtani bhūteṣūccāvaceṣvanu/ praviśṭānyapraviṣṭāni tathā teṣu na teṣvaham// etāvadeva jijñāsyaṃ tattvajijñāsunātmanaḥ/ anvayavyatirekābhyāṃ yatsyāt-sarvatra sarvadā//

46. II.9.33a : ṛte'rthaṃ yatpratīyeta na pratīyeta cātmani/

Energy As Power (*śakti*)

Another important description of the creative energy is as a power (*śakti*) of Bhagavān: "That is truly the power of this Seer which is of the nature of both actual cause and potential effect. It is by this power, that the all-pervading Lord created the universe."[47] The same identification is made in canto eight where Manu prays : "By his own power, which is uncreated he brings about the creation, etc. of the universe. By his eternal knowledge, he sets this power aside and remains actionless."[48] Here there is a two-fold nature within Bhagavān. One, the power, is creative, the other, knowledge, the innermost essence, rests unmoved. Thus the power is the capacity of Bhagavān for being external, while in a truer and deeper sense, his interiority is unchanged and motionless. In another passage the term *śakti* is used of both the interior and the exterior potentialities of Bhagvān, who is "endowed with power of consciousness and of unconsciousness, by whose infinite and unmanifest form all this is pervaded."[49] The power of consciousness is his interior, unchanging essence and the power of unconsciousness is his creative energy, which brings forth the creation of the universe. These two powers by working together constitute the process of the cyclic manifestation and non-manifestation of Bhagavān.

In many places the *Bhāgavata* personifies the first creation of the creative energy as Brahmā, who is the personal aspect of the creative Deity. Through Brahmā the *Bhāgavata*'s abstractions are given a mythical form. Thus in canto one Sūta tells the sages that when the Puruṣa was sleeping on the causal waters "Brahmā the head of the creators of the universe, was born of the lotus of the lake-like navel of the Lord lying on the waters extending his yogic slumber."[50] This theme of Brahmā being self-sprung from the naval of Viṣṇu is the basis for the title 'unborn' and is

47. III.5.25 : sā vā etasya saṃdraṣṭuḥ śaktiḥ sadasadātmikā/māyā nāma mahābhāga yayedaṃ nirmame vibhuḥ//

48. VIII.1.13b : dhatte'sya janmādyajayātmaśaktyā tāṃ vidyayodasya nirīha āste///

49. VII.3.34 : anantāvyaktarūpeṇa yenedamakhilaṃ tatam/ cidacic-chaktiyuktāya tasmai bhagavate namaḥ//

50. I.3.2 : yasyāmbhasi śayānasya yoganidrāṃ vitanvataḥ/ nābhih-radāmbujādāsīdbrahmā viśvasṛjāṃ patiḥ//

common in the *Purāṇas*. After a long meditation he discovers that as the first to be created he is to be responsible for the rest of creation, though under the influence of the creative energy.[51] Yet sages mistake Brahmā for the Lord under the delusive suggestion of the creative energy. Brahmā, in canto two, corrects Nārada: "I manifest the universe, which is already manifested by his self-manifestation, just as the sun, fire, moon, constellations, planets and stars shine due to his splendor...We meditate on him deluded by whose creative energy people call me the guru of the universe."[52]

The *Bhāgavata* extends its concept of creative energy beyond being merely creative. It functions within the sphere of human affairs as a salvific means to the Lord. To the extent that the creation by the creative energy is unreal the devotee takes no delight in it, but to the extent that it is real he is not repulsed by it. The universe created by the creative energy is somthing both to be enjoyed and to be emancipated from, *māyā* being creative first of all and then delusive.[53] The delusive quality of the energy obscures the nature of the reality of the universe: "We, whose intellects are obscured by his creative energy, think that we comprehend the created universe according to our capacity of knowledge."[54] Speculation is vain because it too is under the influence of *māyā*, the energy of Bhagavān, which, while creative, serves his inscrutable purpose.

Yogic Energy

When the Lord wishes to enter into his own creation, which is not reality apart from him, being the product of his creative energy, he draws on a special form of his energy, the mysterious *yogamāyā*. *Yogamāyā* features prominently in the *Bhāgavata*, which is chiefly concerned with narrating the different manifestations and appearances of Bhagavān. *Yogamāyā* is that

51. Cf. II.2.1.

52. II. 5. 11, 12b: yena svarociṣā viśvaṃ rocitaṃ rocayāmyaham/ yathā'rko'gniryathā somo yatharkṣagrahatārakāḥ//...dhīmahi/ yanmāyayā durjayayā māṃ bruvanti jagadgurum//

53. Cf. XI.3.3.

54. II.6.36b : tanmāyayā mohitabuddhayastvidaṃ vinirmitaṃ cātmasamaṃ vicakṣmahe//

aspect of the creative energy which undercuts its delusive aspects. This yogic energy, which is concerned with the appearance of Bhagavān as an *avatāra*, presupposes his metaphysical presence through his creative energy. That he should enter the human sphere presumes in some sense that this presence through the creative energy is insufficient for his purposes. The individual self is limited, its self-understanding obscured by ignorance, yet it is called to devotion to Bhagavān. This call is based upon a divine presence in the universe beyond his creative sustenance of material beings and his identity with the individual self, both of which are the product of the creative energy. The *Bhāgavata* postulates a further form of energy (*māyā*), that is, the yogic energy (*yogamāyā*), which enables Bhagavān to come into contact with his parts, the individual selves, in a human or personal form as the *avatāra*.

The main purpose of the creation by the creative energy is to provide a stage, as it were, for the playful sports (*līlā*) of Bhagavān. As Maitreya says in canto three: "Now I shall recount in due order the sports of Bhagavān, unfolded by his yogic energy for the purposes of the maintenance, creation, and dissolution of the universe."[55] Here the creation, etc. is in some manner connected with the appearance of Bhagavān. The yogic energy, even at the time of the general creation, foresaw the ultimate appearance of Bhagavān in the midst of creation. By means of his yogic energy Kṛṣṇa graces the universe with the beauty of his form: "It was a form useful for the sports of his human forms, a power of his yogic energy. It was the peak of perfect beauty and sublimity, its limbs beautified its ornaments, a wonder even to him."[56] In the same way in canto ten, Bhagavān is compassionate to Śiva's foolishness when he granted Vṛkāsura the power to destroy whatever he touched. In order to rescue Śiva from this dilemma, Bhagavān "assumed the form of a boy by means of his yogic energy and

55. III.5.22 : atha te bhagavallīlā yogamāyopabṛṃhitāḥ/ viśvasthityudbhavāntārthā varṇayāmyanupūrvaśaḥ//

56. III.2.12: yanmartyalīlaupayikaṃ svayogamāyābalaṃ darśyatā gṛhītam/ vismāpanaṃ svasya ca saubhagarddheḥparaṃ padaṃ bhuṣaṇabhūṣaṇāṅgam//

manifested himself at a distance."[57] Thus the yogic energy enables Bhagavān to help his creatures. It is especially connected with Kṛṣṇa's appearance among the cowherd girls of Vṛndāvana. When Kṛṣṇa was born of Devakī in Mathurā, in order to protect him from the wrath of Kaṃsa, his yogic energy took his place. Similarly, his yogic energy was born as a girl to Yaśodā in Vraja, and Vesudeva switched her with Kṛṣṇa, in order to protect Kṛṣṇa. Just as Kaṃsa was about to kill her, the 'yogic energy', the younger sister of Kṛṣṇa, "rose to heaven with eight mighty arms equipped with weapons."[58] His yogic energy assumes forms at opportune times to help Kṛṣṇa, but its most celebrated assistance to Kṛṣṇa takes place during the ecstatic play (*rāsalīlā*) of Kṛṣṇa with the cowherd girls in the tenth canto: "On those nights adorned with blooming autumnal jasmines, glorious Bhagavān decided to sport, supported by his yogic energy."[59] This yogic energy is responsible for the extraordinary aura surrounding these events. The ecstatic play takes place in a half-real, half-magic realm. Kṛṣṇa is the master of yogic power. He is called a *yogin*, *yogeśvara*, a master of yoga, and a *yogeśvareśvara*, a master of the masters of yoga.[60] By means of his yogic energy, Kṛṣṇa replicates himself and dances personally with each of the many cowherd girls simultaneously.[61] Kṛṣṇa's playful pastimes are for his own pleasure and that of his creatures. Non-dualism is preserved by the mediation of this special form of the creative energy, the yogic energy which manifests Bhagavān on the basis of the creation by the creative energy. The same energy which creates also maintains not just the existence but also the purity of Bhagavān's creation. By means of the creative energy Bhagavān guarantees justice. Finally the creative energy allows Bhagavān to sport in an unrestrained revelry without in any way marring his pure non-dualism.

57. X.88.27 : taṃ tathāvyasanaṃ draṣṭvā bhagavānvṛjinārdanaḥ/ dūrāt-pratyudiyādbhūtvā baṭuko yogamāyayā//

58. X.4.9 : sā taddhastātsamutpatya sadyo devyambaraṃ gatā/ adṛśya-tānujā viṣṇoḥ sāyudhāṣṭamahābhujā//

59. X.29.1 : bhagavānapi tā rātrīḥ śaradotphullamallikāḥ/ vīkṣya rantuṃ manaścakre yogamāyāmupāśritaḥ//

60. Cf. X.29.16 and X.29.42.

61. Cf. X.33.3.

Illusion and Bondage

Though *māyā* is very often translated and thought of as illusory energy or illusion, the citations from the *Bhāgavata* thus far have indicated that it should be thought of primarily as creative energy, and in certain contexts, as yogic energy. However, the *Bhāgavata* does use *māyā* in its sense as illusion, though the context never allows it to be regarded as separate from its source in Bhagavān.

In canto four Bhṛgu says that self-knowledge is obscured by Bhagavān's illusory energy (*māyā*): "Brahmā and other embodied beings have been deprived of knowledge of Self by the impenetrable creative energy and sleep in darkness; they do not know your real nature which permeates their own self.[62] In canto three Maitreya tells Vidura that bondage is due to the creative energy: "It is the creative energy of Bhagavān, which is against all logic. Hence the afflictio n and bondage to (the soul who is essentially) free from bondage."[63] Because of the creative energy the individual self appears to be bound, just as a man might see himself beheaded in a dream, but there is really no bondage. The bondage is rooted in the creative energy, which allows ignorance to obscure Bhagavān's creation of the universe. The creative energy has its own purposes and thus grants or withholds liberating knowledge. Both bondage and liberation are grounded in the same reality. As Kṛṣṇa tells Uddhava in canto eleven : "O highly intelligent, although I am one, it is in relation to the individual self that the eternal bondage exists due to ignorance, the opposite state due to knowledge."[64] Because of his non-dual nature, Bhagavān, being beyond change, is above bondage and liberation, but his forms, the individual selves created by his creative energy, succumb to bondage and liberation as he wishes. A return to Bhagavān of his evolved

62. IV.7.30 : yanmāyayā gahanayāpahṛtātmabodhā brahmādayastanubhṛtastamasi svapantaḥ/ nātman śritaṃ tava vidantyadhunāpi tattvaṃ so'yaṃ prasīdatu bhavānpraṇatātmabandhuḥ//

63. III.7.9 : seyaṃ bhagavato māyā yannayena virudhyate/ īśvarasya vimuktasya kārpaṇyamuta bandhanam//

64. XI.11.4 : ekasyaiva mamāṁśasya jīvasyaiva mahāmate/ bandho' syāvidyayā'nādirvidyayā ca tathetaraḥ//

forms, the individual selves is premised upon a greater realization of their non-duality with the Lord. This is accomplished by a negation or retraction of the creative energy.[65] Then birth and death and rebirth will be no more and liberation is accomplished: "He is realized as the highest bliss of meditation by the negation of the creative energy which creates all distinctions and differences."[66]

This discussion of the different texts on the role of the creative energy serves to illustrate the complexity of the relation between Bhagavān, the universe, and the individual self. However, it is clear that the *Bhāgavata* does not use *māyā* in the same sense that Śaṃkara and the *māyāvādins* do. The language and similies used are similar because both drew on the Upaniṣads and Vedāntic material for their sources. This question is summarized by T. Hopkins :

> The relation of *māyā* to the supreme being is stressed in the *Bhāgavata*, in contrast to the later denial of any ontological connection. The phenomenal world is the definite creation of Bhagavān, the highest soul or Brahman, who creates the world in sport by his power of *māyā*. The world is like a dream only in the sense that it is dependent on a creator without whom it would not exist; it is insubstantial only by comparison to the supreme Lord who is the source of its existence. Perception of the world is not the result of *avidyā*; it is rather its cause, since the phenomenal world obscures true knowledge of the Lord.[67]

Non-dualism and Pluralism

The non-duality of the Bhagavān with the universe and the individual self is not the non-dualism without qualities (*nirviśeṣādvaita* or *abhedavāda*) of Śaṃkara. The *Bhāgavata*'s teaching is a non-dualism compatible with a plurality of beings and

65. Cf. I.15.30-31.

66. VI.4.28a : sa vai mamāśeṣaviśeṣamāyāniṣedhanirvāṇasukhānubhūtiḥ/

67. Hopkins, "The Vaishṇava Bhakti Movement in the *Bhāgavata Purāṇa*," p. 84-85.

individual selves. At the end of canto ten there is a chapter which deals directly with this relationship. Parīkṣit wonders how the Scripture immersed in and dealing with the qualities (*guṇa*) can then know about a God who is indefinable, without qualities, and beyond cause and effect.[68] Sūta in reply asserts that the creation is indeed from Bhagavān, however transcendent he may be. He created so that the individuals so evolved might delight in his creation and at the same time return to him in liberation.[69] Ignorance, paradoxically, is beginningless and has assumed the qualities for an evil purpose. But Bhagavān, though transcendent, has many divine attributes. There is delusion, no doubt ultimately derived from Bhagavān himself, which regards the qualities as not derived from Bhāgavān. But the qualities of the universe, which are described in the Scriptures, can only point to Bhagavān, whether in an exterior manifested state or in an interior unmanifest state: "The wise recognize that the universe that is perceived is you, because you always persist and because it is just as the clay remains constant though its modifications are made and unmade."[70] Therefore words can describe and the mind can know the transcendent Bhagavān since everything is Brahman and anything that can exist even for a time is part of him, whatever can be thought or spoken refers to him.

Although he is the ultimate reality, who is without difference (*abheda*), the Brahman evolves from himself and enters into the categories of creation and becomes differentiated.[71] What is more, Brahman has become personal within the created universe in order to show mortals the truth of that creation. The microcosm is like the macrocosm, one, undivided, and personal: "...your manifestations have revealed the true nature of your Self, which is difficult to realize."[72] The reality of the universe is relative to the reality of the Self: "All the universe, a threefold product of the cosmic mind, appears as real due to

68. Cf. X.87.1

69. Cf. X.87.2-3.

70. X.87.15a : bṛhadupalabdhametadavayantyavaśeṣatayā yata udayāstamayau vikṛtermṛdivā'vikṛtāt//

71. Cf. X.87.17.

72. X.87.21a : duravagamātmatattvanigamāya tavāttatanoścaritamahāmṛtābdhiparivartapariśramaṇāḥ/

the superimposition of the unreal on you. Those who know the Self regard this universe as real because it is their Self. Just as persons seeking gold do not discard its modifications as they are essentially gold, the knowers of the Self conclude that the universe is their very Self as he made it and entered into it."[73] Both the individual self and the universe are identical because both have their source in the Highest Self. The mind can indeed 'penetrate to Brahman, even though he is without qualities and indefinable."[74] Non-duality is the import of the *Bhāgavata*, yet the universe is not thereby unreal. Both the universe and the individual self have a degree of reality derived from Brahman with whom they are not different. It may be that the redactor of the *Bhāgavata* was unable to present a clear scholastic understanding of this paradox, as the later Vaiṣṇava *ācāryas* were to attempt. Nonetheless, he knew what his faith was and held firmly to its paradoxes.

73. X.87.26 : sadiva manastrivṛttvayi vibhātyasadāmanujātsadabhimṛś-antyaśeṣamidamātmatayātmavidaḥ/ na hi vikṛtiṃ tyajanti kanakasya tadāt-matayā svakṛtamanupraviṣṭamidamātmatayā vasitam//

74. X.87.49b : yathā brahmaṇyanirdeśye nirguṇe'pi manaścaret//

CHAPTER III

THE SĀṂKHYA OF THE *BHĀGAVATA*

We have stated in Chapter II that the *Bhāgavata*, in addition to its basic use of Upaniṣadic language, also employs the terminology of Sāṃkhya. Both Sāṃkhya and Vedānta have their roots in the *Upaniṣads*. The main thrust of both was the insight of non-dualism. With the passage of time the tradition of Sāṃkhya took a dualistic and non-theistic, if not atheistic, turn, in the *Sāṃkhya Kārikās* of Īśvarakṛṣṇa. The Vaiṣṇava *Purāṇas* have preserved a primitive Sāṃkhya which is theistic and compatible with the Vedāntic non-dualism of Brahman and the world, and of the Highest Self and the individual self. In the *Bhāgavata Purāṇa* the Purāṇic Sāṃkhya is correlative to and corroborative of non-dualism. An investigation of its Sāṃkhya passages reenforces the conclusion that the non-dualism of the *Bhāgavata* is able to accommodate the pluralism of the world and of the individual selves.

Kapila, the legendary founder of the Sāṃkhya school, is in the *Bhāgavata* an avatāra of Bhagavān, who was born into the house of Kardama in order to found the Sāṃkhya system: "In this world, this birth of mine is for the exposition of the true knowledge of the categories leading to self-realization for those who seek liberation from the subtle body."[1] The intent of the redactor of the *Bhāgavata* is obviously to reenforce his teaching by appeal to the traditional authority of the Sāṃkhya of Kapila. Even though Sāṃkhya terminology is found throughout the *Bhāgavata*, Sāṃkhya itself is presented as a special

1. III.24.36: etanme janma loke'sminmumukṣūnāṃ durāśayāt/ prasaṃkhyānāya tattvānāṃ saṃmatāyātmadarśane//

revelation by Kapila to his mother Devahūti in canto three and by Kṛṣṇa to Uddhava in canto eleven. This chapter will focus on those passages.

Sāṃkhya is both a cosmology and a psychology. It traces from a single principle the evolution of the entire universe and of the consciousness of the Individual person. In the *Bhāgavata* that single principle is Brahman: "Primal nature (*prakṛti*) is the material cause of what is real. The Highest Person is its support. Time is its revealer. I, Brahman, constitute these three."[2]

Brahman or Bhagavān by his own power creates all beings within his Self, without being changed in any way, just as a spider spins a web out of its own substance and then plays in it.[3] In the beginning he was all alone beyond the constituent qualities. All potentiality was submerged within him in a latent equilibrium. Intent on becoming many, Bhagavān by means of his creative energy brought forth from his own being time, the inherited destiny of creatures (*karma*), and their innate essence (*svabhāva*).[4] These had formerly been manifest but had become latent and now were again approaching manifestation. These innate principles enable Bhagavān to reflect his unity in the plurality of other beings. "The peculiarity of the *Bhāgavata*," according to A. Sen Gupta, "lies in the fact that here the supreme self, on its own initiative, has reflected itself in *Māyā* and thus fallen under the influence of its own power."[5] This is not the case in the classical Sāṃkhya where the motive for creation is inherent in primal nature (*prakṛti*) and not in a transcendent reality.

The two versions of Sāṃkhya have much in common, yet also have significant differences.[6] According to the *Bhāgavata*, the first emergent category is the primal nature (*prakṛti*) from which evolves the great principle (*mahat*) which contains within

2. XI.24.19 : prakṛtirhyasyopādānamādhāraḥ puruṣaḥ paraḥ/ sato' bhivyañjakaḥ kālo brahma tattritayaṃ tvaham//

3. Cf. II.5.5

4. Cf. II.5.21.

5. Anima Sen Gupta, *The Evolution of the Samkhya School of Thought* (Patna : Pioneer Press, 1959), p. 98.

6. Cf. chart in Appendix I, pp. 149-50.

itself the germ of the entire universe. The great principle has a nature of pure being and intelligence adequate for the entire cosmos. The great principle of the *Bhāgavata* is not the intellect (*buddhi*) of Īśvarakṛṣṇa's classical Sāṃkhya where it is the source for the bondage of the individual spirit (*puruṣa*) nor does the evolution of the great principle occur because of the presence of unbound individual spirits as in Īśvarakṛṣṇa.[7] Rather the great principle of the *Bhāgavata* is the cosmic intelligence (*citta*) of the cosmic Person (*puruṣa*): "Then, under the impelling force of time, the great principle (*mahat*) was generated from the unmanifest (=*māyā*). It is of the nature of intelligence (*vijñāna*) which dispels inertia (*tamas*) and manifests the universe lying within the body of the self."[8] In the *Bhāgavata*, in contrast to Īśvarakṛṣṇa, the phenomenal intellect or mind (*buddhi*) is a function of the individual self and is an evolute of the 'active' ego (*rāsjasa ahaṃkāra*).

From the great principle the three-fold ego (*ahaṃkāra*) evolves, the source of 'I' and 'mine.' The three forms of the ego are the 'knowing' ego (*sāttvika*), the 'active' ego (*rājasa*), and the 'inertial' ego (*tāmasa*). From the 'knowing' ego arises the mind (*manas*), "characterized by thinking and special meditation and is the source of desire."[9] The mind is directive, supervising and motivating the senses. From the 'active' ego the phenomenal mind (*buddhi*) arises, which is a collective term for the functioning of the cognitive (*jñāna*) and

7. Cf. the *Sāṃkhya Kārikās* of Iśvarakṛṣṇa XXIII and XXXV: adhyavasāyo buddhirdharmo jñānaṃ virāga aiśvaryam/ sāttivkametadrūpaṃ tāmasamasmādviparyastam// "Intellect is determinative. Virtue, wisdom, non-attachment, and the possession of lordly powers constitute its pure being form; the reverse of these are of its inertial form." sāntaḥ karaṇā buddhiḥ sarvaṃ viṣayamavagāhate yasmāt/ tasmāttrividhaṃ karaṇaṃ dvāri dvārāṇi śeṣāṇi// "For the reason that the intellect with the other internal organs ascertains the nature of objects of sense, the internal organs are the principal ones, while the rest are the entrances thereto." The translations are by S. S. Suryanarayana Sastri in *A Sourcebook in Indian Philosophy*, edited by Sarvepalli Radhakrishnan and Charles A. Moore (Princeton : Princeton University Press, 1957), pp. 434 and 437.

8. III.5.27 : tato'bhavanmahattattvamavyaktātkālacoditāt/ vijñānātmātmadehasthaṃ viśvaṃ vyañjaṃstamonudaḥ//

9. III.26.27b : yatsaṃkalpavikalpābhyāṃ vartate kāmasaṃbhavaḥ//

the conative (*karma*) senses (*indriya*). The phenomenal mind is characterized by doubt, misapprehension, correct apprehension, memory and sleep.[10] From the 'inertial' ego the subtle elements (*tanmātra*) and the gross elements (*bhūta*) arise. In classical Sāṃkhya the 'active' ego activates and coordinates the other two phases of the ego. It has no evolutes of its own.[11] in the *Bhāgavata*'s scheme of evolution, each phase of the ego has its own particular evolutes. Thus the evolution of the categories from the great principle down to the gross elements encompasses all of manifest reality, both material and psychic.

In canto eleven the *Bhāgavata* acknowledges the existence of several schools of Sāṃkhya which enumerate the categories differently.[12] Irenically the *Bhāgavata* accepts each of these schools by declaring that there was no real difference among the several accounts. Since cause and effect are substantially identical in a Sāṃkhya system different ways of enumerating the categories are possible. If one considers that spirit (*puruṣa*), under the influence of ignorance, cannot attain liberation by its own efforts, he may then affirm the need for a Supreme Person, a higher spiritual principle, and will number twenty-six categories instead of twenty-five. Therefore the *Bhāgavata* accepts both: "As there is the possibility of offering a reason for the causal relations of these categories as well as their enumeration as advanced by the disputants, according to their capacity of argumentation, we accept the position presented by them."[13]

It is important to remember that the evolution of the categories (*tattva*), according to the *Bhāgavata*, takes place at the start of a cosmic cycle which proceeds to dissolution. This dissolution, or devolution, is also described in terms of the

10. Cf. III.26.29b-30.

11. Cf. the *Sāṃkhya Kārikās* XXV : sāttvika ekādaśakaḥ pravartate vaikṛtādahaṅkārāt/ bhūtādestanmātraḥ sa tāmasastaijasādubhayam// "The 'set of eleven' abounding in the *sattva* attribute evolves out of the *vaikṛta* form of the 'I-principle'; the set of rudimentary substances from the *bhūtādi* form of the 'I-principle'; and both of them from the *taijasa* form of the 'I-principle." pp. 434-35.

12. Cf. XI.22.2-3a.

13. XI.22.9 : paurvāparyamato'mīṣāṁ prasaṃkhyānamabhīpsatām/ yathā viviktaṃ yadvaktraṃ gṛhṇīmo yuktisaṃbhavāt //

categories. The gross elements revert to the subtle elements, which in turn revert to the 'inertial' ego. Similarly the cognitive and conative senses revert to the 'active' ego, and the mind reverts to the 'knowing' ego. Both the material and the psychic realms, which are functions of each other, devolve to a state of latency in the great principle at the same time. "The great principle, endowed with qualities, is withdrawn into the qualities which in turn are dissolved into the unmanifest (*prakṛti*). That unmanifest is withdrawn into time which has ceased to function."[14] Time reverts to the cosmic Person, who rules by means of his creative energy. Finally everything is merged into the Self, who stands alone.

Contrary to Īśvarakṛṣṇa's Sāṃkhya where there are many spirits (*puruṣa*),[15] in the *Bhāgavata* there is only one Person (*puruṣa*), who is Supreme, "the Self, who is beginningless, without qualities, and beyond primal nature."[16] In this Sāṃkhya scheme of non-dualism, the *puruṣa* is that aspect of Bhagavān which transcends primal nature and is without its qualities, yet ensouls primal nature and all its evolutes. He does this of his own free will in a sportful manner. In one sense the Person is ensnared by the possibilities of primal nature, whose charms obscure his consciousness so that he becomes many individual spirits.[17] God, as it were, while remaining beyond his creation, chooses to be evolved into it, and to have his single essence obscured by multiplicity. The Person is therefore not on an equal level with primal nature, divided by a dualist abyss, as in classical Sāṃkhya, but as a higher form of Bhagavān possesses primal

14. XI.24.26 : sa līyate mahānsveṣu guṇeṣu guṇavattamaḥ/te'vyakte saṃpralīyante tatkāle līyate'vyaye//

15. Cf. the *Sāṃkhya Kārikās* XVIII : janana maraṇakaraṇānāṃ pratiniyamādayugapatpravṛtteśca/ puruṣabahutvaṃ siddhaṃ traiguṇyaviparyayāccaiva// "The plurality of spirits certainly follows from the distributive nature of the incidence of birth and death and of the endowment of the instruments of cognition and action, from bodies engaging in action, not all at the same time, and also from differences in the proportion of the three qualities." p. 432.

16. III.26.3a : anādirātmā puruṣo nirguṇaḥ prakṛteḥ paraḥ /

17. Cf. III.26.4-5.

nature, which is thus not an independent principle. Primal nature from which all else is derived is itself derived.[18]

The Sāṃkhya scheme of evolution is built on the principle of *satkārya*, according to which "the real entity at the basis of the product is that which the earlier existence adopts as the material to evolve the later existence, or that which is, in a given case, considered to be the beginning and the end of a certain effect."[19] There is no ultimate distinction between cause and effect, or between power and the possessor of the power. Each category, except for the gross elements, which are the final evolutes, is both a substance and a power, an evolute and an evolver. Each category has no quality not already present in the category it evolved from. That which is gross has a subtle form within that which produced it. This principle applies for the primal nature in relation to the Person as well as for the gross elements in relation to the subtle elements. According to the principle of *satkārya*, in the words of Sen Gupta, "whatever is non-existent cannot be brought into existence and ...whatever is existent cannot be made totally non-existent ...The effect that is produced from the cause is not totally dissimilar to it, as no intercourse is possible between two absolutely distinct entities."[20] Thus the effect is always subtly present in the cause. Since there is ultimately one cause, all that is, is present in that one cause.

Having so firmly grounded multiplicity in unity by the doctrine of *satkārya*, how does the *Bhāgavata* explain the transformation (*pariṇāma*) of unity into multiplicity? How is that equilibrium of the qualities within the unmanifest (*prakṛti*) disturbed? In the second canto Brahmā asserts that "it is due to the presence or direction of the Person that time became the cause of the imbalance in the three qualities, that the innate es-

18. Cf. the *Sāṃkhya Kārikās* LXIII : rūpaiḥ saptabhirevaṃ badhnātyātmānamātmanā prakṛtiḥ/ saiva ca puruṣasyārthaṃ prati vimocayatyekarūpeṇa// "Primal nature by herself binds herself by means of seven forms; and by means of one form she causes deliverance for the benefit of the spirit." p. 444.

19. XI.24.18 : yadupādāya pūrvastu bhāvo vikurute param/ ādiranto yadā yasya tatsatyamabhidhīyate//

20. Sen Gupta, *The Evolution of the Samkya School of Thought*, p. 41.

sence is the cause of their modifications, and that inherited destiny (*karma*) is the cause of the birth of the great principle."[21] These three, time, the innate essence of creature, and their inherited destiny, are not categories (*tattva*) in the usual sense, dependent upon the primal nature, but powers (*śakti*) of Bhagavān. Nor are they products of the evolutionary process, which presuppose these supraphenomenal powers. In fact the powers are identified with Bhagavān.

Time, which is sometimes designated as the twenty-fifth category, is identified with Bhagavān : "that is designated time which sets in motion the undifferentiated qualities of primal nature which were in a state of equilibrium."[22] Bhagavān, who is unaffected by change, by means of his creative energy dwells within all his creatures in the form of the Person and outside them in the form of time. The *Bhāgavata* sees time in three ways : (1) as God, (2) as his power, and (3) as temporal sequence.[23] Time as God and as his power presides not only over the disturbance of the equilibrium of the qualities, but also over the maintenance and dissolution of the universe. Creation has a beginning and an end, but time has neither beginning nor end, nor does it change, since it is an integral part of the nature of the Supreme Deity.[24] "One might say," with Bhaṭṭācārya, "somewhat paradoxically that Time is free from the limitations of time."[25]

Time, the innate essence of creature, and their inherited destiny are eternal functions of the Deity. In the *Bhāgavata* there is no creation from nothing nor does time begin. Thus the creature, whether latent or manifest, always has an innate essence by which he may become manifest and always has an inherited destiny which will determine the precise details of that manifestation. The innate essence is Bhagavān's purpose and determination for each existent, modified only by the inherited destiny of the individual self, both of which are present to Bhagavān before

21. II.5.22 : kālādguṇavyatikaraḥ pariṇāmaḥ svabhāvataḥ/ karmaṇo janma mahataḥ puruṣādhiṣṭhitādabhūt//

22. III.26.17 : parkṛterguṇasāmyasya nirviśeṣasya mānavi/ ceṣṭhā yataḥ sa bhagavānkāla ityupalakṣitaḥ/

23. Cf. X.16.41.

24. Cf. IV. 11.19.

25. Bhaṭṭācārya, *The Philosophy of the Śrimad-Bhāgavata*, I,259.

any particular creation, since the cycle of death and rebirth (*saṃsāra*) is eternal. Bhagavān sports for the purpose of giving the individual self existence and that sport, by his will, is subject to the innate essence of the individual self. It is also subject to the free actions of the individual self (*karma*). These two, the innate essence and the inherited destiny of the individual self, are identified with Bhagavān himself in accordance with the non-dualism of the *Bhāgavata*.[26]

The individual self (*jīva*) for whom creation occurs is a shadow of the Supreme Person. As a function of the Person the individual self is not essentially tied down to the phenomenal products of the evolution from primal nature. The senses, the objects of the senses, and the mind constitute the body of the individual self which must give them up.[27] The individual self is eternal, immutable, pure, one, a witness, the refuge, unchanging, self-luminous, a cause, all-pervasive, unattached and perfect,[28] qualities which it shares with the Supreme Self, because it is identical with that Self. The individual self achieves phenomenal existence when the Person (*puruṣa*) and the primal nature (*prakṛti*) meet. The result of their meeting is the limitation of the Self in a body, that is, the individual self. Thus the individual self cannot really die for "...the Self is unborn and does not die."[29] When the body dies the individual self is reunited with Brahman. This is one of the more extreme identity texts of the *Bhāgavata* where the empirical and phenomenal self only appears to differ from Brahman.

S. Dasgupta discerns a difference in emphasis between the Sāṃkhya texts in cantos two and three and those in canto eleven. The latter tend to an unqualified monism rather than a qualified non-dualism. Thus Dasgupta says that

> ...though the two treatments may not be interpreted as radically different, yet the monistic tendency which regards all worldly experiences as illusory is so remarkably

26. Cf. III.29.36.
27. Cf. XI.13.25-26.
28. Cf. VII.7.19.
29. XII.5.4...tata ātmā hyajo'maraḥ//

stressed that it very nearly destroys the realistic note which is a special feature of the Sāṃkhya schools of thought.[30]

In canto eleven, for example, Kṛṣṇa tells Uddhava to "please understand that it is merely an illusion which shows difference which is reflected in the self due to ignorance about its true nature."[31] The world is an illusion and the individual self in it is dreaming even in his waking state. The only solution is to resort to Sāṃkhya and Yoga, because "a person who has mastered Yoga's samādhi and has realized reality does not resort to the dream-like unreal world any more than an awakened person to the objects in a dream."[32] The goal of Sāṃkhya is Bhagavān himself. It is almost as if the body had a greater reality than its possessor, the individual self, which is really the Self deluded by the products of the creative energy and limited by the body.

For the *Bhāgavata* the question of bondage is not minimized and release from it is a pressing concern, in spite of those passages which seem to describe the world and the individual self as illusory.[33] As Sanatkumāra says in canto four: "In this world, there is no worse loss of his self-interest for a person than the loss of his own Self for whose sake every other thing in the world becomes dear."[34] Liberation alone is a worthy end of life since any other purpose is subject to the dread of death and rebirth. Liberation is one of the distinguishing characteristics of a *Purāṇa*[35] and is the goal of the process of Sāṃkhya and Yoga. But just as in the lists of the characteristics of a *Puraṇā* liberation is subordinated to 'support' (*āśraya*), so the process which leads to liberation is subordinated to the process which leads to 'support', that is, devotion. Liberation is proper to an impersonal non-dualism, while devotion characterizes a personal non-dualism. Thus in canto eleven Bhagavān says that "Neither

30. Dasgupta, *A History of Indian Philosophy*, IV, 32.

31. XI.22.56b : ātmāgrahaṇanirbhātaṃ paśya vaikalpikaṃ bhramam//

32. XI.13.37b : taṃ saprapañcamadhirūḍhasamādhiyogaḥ svāpnaṃ punarna bhajate pratibuddhavastuḥ//

33. Cf. Sen Gupta, *The Evolution of the Samkhya School of Thought*, p. 41.

34. IV.22.32 : nātaḥ parataro loke puṃsaḥ svārthavyatikramaḥ/ yadadhyanyasya preyastvamātmanaḥ svavyatikramāt//

35. Cf. II.10.1.

Sāṃkhya nor Yoga nor Dharma nor the study of the Veda, nor austerities nor renunciation leads a person to me as does intensive devotion."[36]

Devotion profoundly alters the context of the *Bhāgavata*'s treatment of Sāṃkhya. That Sāṃkhya indeed corroborates the non-dualism derived from Vedāntic sources. It even takes an extreme monistic form in some passages. Yet the highest wisdom of the *Bhāgavata,* its clearest vision, lies in its teaching of devotion to Bhagavān Kṛṣṇa, a teaching which qualifies its non-dualism. Thus its Sāṃkhya is compatible for the most part with both the *Bhāgavata*'s non-dualism and its theism. It provides a theoretic framework for binding the two together in a clear vision. The next chapter will show that the identification of Kṛṣṇa as Bhagavān is a key element influencing that vision.

36. XI.14.20 : na sādhayati māṃ yogo na sāṃkhyam dharma uddhava/ na svādhyāyastapastyāgo yathā bhaktirmamorjitā//

CHAPTER IV

THE IDENTITY OF BHAGAVĀN

Kṛṣṇa Over Viṣṇu

By means of its non-dualism the *Bhāgavata* sought to provide a firm basis for a religious devotion to the Supreme Deity. In the history of Bhāgavatism and Vaiṣṇavism the *Bhāgavata Purāṇa*, although a late piece of literature, gives a conclusive resolution to the problem of the personality of the Supreme Deity for all those schools of Vaiṣṇavism which regard it as authoritative. The Deity of later Bhāgavatism had an inclusive quality which enabled him to absorb many local deities and cults. It did this through the doctrine of the divine manifestations (*avatāra*) to which is to be attributed much of Bhāgavatism's popularity. "The syncretism effected through this doctrine," in the words of S. Jaiswal, "was sometimes brāhmaṇical and sometimes popular in character, but to a great extent it was the reconciliatory attitude of Vaiṣṇavism which gave the country a kind of cultural unity and succeeded in establishing the same kind of social structure all over India."[1] The *Bhāgavata Purāṇa* played an important role in this process.

For the *Bhāgavata*, which is inclusive of popular deities, who the Supreme Deity is and what his name signifies is of decisive importance. Undoubtedly L. Shinn is correct when he says that as "one reads the *Bhāgavata* he may be confused about the divinity which lies somewhere behind all the names given to him."[2]

1. Suvira Jaiswal, *The Origin and Development of Vaiṣṇavism* (Delhi : Munshiram Manoharlal, 1967), p. 132.
2. Shinn, "Kṛṣṇa's *Līlā* : An Analysis of the Relationship of the Notion of Deity and the Concept of *Saṃsāra* in the *Bhāgavata Purāṇa*," p. 94.

But as one reads further in the *Bhāgavata*, especially in its climactic tenth canto, there is little doubt who Bhagavān is, namely Kṛṣṇa, although the relationship between all the manifestations, deities, and Bhagavān's many epithets is far from clear, as would be expected in the Purāṇic genre. It becomes clear that the personality of Bhagavān Kṛṣṇa subordinates to itself the titles and identities of Viṣṇu, Nārāyaṇa, Puruṣa, Īśvara, Hari, Vāsudeva, Janārdana, etc. The pervasive theme, then, of the *Bhāgavata Purāṇa* is the identification of Bhagavān with Kṛṣṇa.

The history of the gradual assimilation by Viṣṇu of the characters of Nārāyaṇa and Vāsudeva-Kṛṣṇa is obscure and much disputed by scholars. The title 'Bhagavān' originally was associated with Nārāyaṇa and through him became connected with Viṣṇu.[3] The meeting of Bhagavān Viṣṇu-Nārāyaṇa with the personality of Vāsudeva-Kṛṣṇa resulted in the doctrine of the divine manifestations, avatāras and vyūhas, which centered on the manifestation of Kṛṣṇa. At least one redactor of the *Mahābhārata* brought to the fore the Kṛṣṇa manifestation of Viṣṇu. With the *Harivaṃśa* and the *Viṣṇu Purāṇa* the stories of the child and cowherder Kṛṣṇa are introduced into the literary tradition, enhancing his personality, but there is still no doubt in these books that the manifestation of Kṛṣṇa is a descent (*avatāra*) of the Supreme Deity Viṣṇu. By the time of the writing of the *Bhāgavata* in the ninth century, their roles have been reversed and Bhagavān no longer refers primarily to Viṣṇu but to Kṛṣṇa. An examination of the text of the *Bhāgavata* will illustrate this transformation, which laid the foundation for the rise of emotional devotion in later Hinduism.

The Four Ages

In the eleventh canto there is a description of the roles of the Deity in the four ages: "Keśava in the ages of Kṛta, Tretā,

3. Jaiswal, *The Origin and Development of Vaiṣṇavism*, p. 38. This is contrary to the common assertion that the title 'Bhagavān' associated with the Vaiṣnava deities was originally a title of Kṛṣṇa Vāsudeva. See H. C. Raychaudhury, *Materials for the Study of the Early History of the Vaishṇava Sect* (New Delhi: Oriental Books Reprint Corporation, 1975/1920), p. 60ff. and Jitendranath Banerjea, *Paurāṇic and Tāntric Religion* (*Early Phase*) Calcutta : University Press, 1966), p. 21.

Dvāpara, and Kali assumes complexions, names, and forms, and is worshipped in different ways."[4] The Deity is known as Haṃsa, Suparna, Vaikuṇṭha, Dharma, Yogeśvara, Amala, Īśvara, Puruṣa, Avyakta, and Paramātma. These are the titles of Viṣṇu, although they could be applied to any deity. In the Kṛta age the Deity has a white complexion and four arms. In the Tretā age he has a crimson hue and appears in the form of sacrifices. Pious men worship with the Vedic forms and Hari is the embodiment of the gods. In the Dvāpara age the Lord has a dark complexion, wears the Kaustubha gem and the Śrīvatsa curl. Men worship by means of both Vedic and Tantric rituals and seek the Supreme Reality in a human form with the marks of a king. In the Kali age the *Vedas* are neglected and Bhagavān is worshipped by the Tantric practices of chanting and singing his name.[5] Even though Kṛṣṇa lived in the Dvāpara age, there is a special blessing for those born in the Kali age, which begins at Kṛṣṇa's death. A the world runs down in the various ages, each succeeding age is in greater need of the Supreme Deity's presence. While these ages are a traditional device to show that the universe is running down, the *Bhāgavata* uses them to show the value and importance of the Supreme Deity in his Kṛṣṇa aspect, who is more and more present as the universe degenerates.

In the Kali age, which begins with Kṛṣṇa's death, people delight in sin. Sin could not enter the world until Kṛṣṇa had left it; the two are incompatible. But as Kṛṣṇa's physical presence departs his memory takes on a new importance : "O King, indeed there is one great quality in the Kali age, which is a storehouse of faults, since by chanting about Kṛṣṇa attachment is loosened and a person reaches the Highest."[6] What was attained in the other ages by meditating on Viṣṇu, by sacrifices, or by worship, in the Kali age is attained through chanting and singing. Thus the remembrance and celebration of Bhagavān Kṛṣṇa is as important for liberation and final beatitude as his physical presence as an *avatāra*, perhaps, as we shall see later, more so.

4. XI.5.20 : kṛtaṃ tretā dvāparaṃ ca kalirityeṣu keśavaḥ/ nānāvarṇābhidhākāro nānaiva vidhinejyate //

5. Cf. XI.5.24-26.

6. XII.3.51 : kalerdoṣanidhe rājannasti hyeko mahānguṇaḥ/ kīrtanādeva kṛṣṇasya muktasaṅgaḥ paraṃ vrajet//

Kṛṣṇa's death and departure is the blessed occasion for the appearance of the *Bhāgavata,* which "benefits those who have been blinded in the Kali age."[7]

The special revelation of Bhagavān's glories and activities among men in the different ages made to the sages by the *Bhāgavata* enables them to love and devote themselves to Bhagavān in a way more intense than was ever before possible. The *Purāṇa* of the devotees of Bhagavān, the *Bhāgavata,* extends his presence in the Kali age and functions as an *avatāra* on the behalf of men oppressed by the absence of Bhagavān. Indeed the *Bhāgavata Mahātmya* from the *Padma Purāṇa* identifies Bhagavān and the *Bhāgavata*: "The sages come to regard the holy book of the *Bhāgavata* as a form of Bhagavān (*bhagavad-rūpam*) in the Kali age and capable of conferring the reward of speedy access to Vaikuṇṭha by being read or heard."[8] Later on the *Mahātmya* describes the *Bhāgavata* as consisting of Brahman (*brahmātmaka*).[9] If the singing and hearing of the stories of Bhagavān in all his manifestations is conducive to liberation, it must be necessary that the primary subject of those stories be the Supreme Being. There is little doubt that this is the intent of the redactor of the *Bhāgavata* when he narrates the stories of Kṛṣṇa or the stories of Viṣṇu's descents which are related to Kṛṣṇa. In effect he so identifies Kṛṣṇa with Viṣṇu as to replace Viṣṇu with Kṛṣṇa as the primary personality of the Supreme Deity. This conversion of Viṣṇu into Kṛṣṇa by the *Bhāgavata* has had great influence on the nature of the devotional life of the Vaiṣṇavas ever since.

The Questions of the Sages

In the first canto the sages ask questions of Sūta, the answers to which comprise the *Bhāgavata.* Four of those questions, or requests, have a bearing on this problem of the relation between Viṣṇu and Kṛṣṇa. The first question the sages ask Sūta is to

7. I.3.45b : kalau naṣṭadṛśāmeṣa purāṇārko'dhunoditaḥ//

8. *Bhāgavata Mahātmya* I. 20 : menire bhagavadrūpaṃ śāstraṃ bhāgavataṃ kalau/ paṭhanācchravaṇāt sadyo vaikuṇṭhaphaladāyakam //

9. Cf. *Bhāgavata Mahātmya* III.74a.

draw out the essence of the Scriptures from the confusion of differing assertions which perplex the sages. They seek their true import. The second question seeks to know why "Bhagavān, the Lord of the Sātvatas, was born of Devakī, Vasudeva's wife."[10] The son of Devakī was Kṛṣṇa, thus identifying Kṛṣṇa with Bhagavān. The third question seeks to know the story of "the noble actions, which have been told by the great seers, of him who for sport assumes forms (*kala*)."[11] The third question refers to the various appearances of Bhagavān, traditionally thought of as the manifestations of Viṣṇu. The fourth question centers again on Kṛṣṇa : "O wise one, therefore describe the auspicious narratives of Hari's manifestations (*avatāra*), who performed sports of his own will by means of his creative energy."[12] The sages are never sated with hearing stories of Kṛṣṇa and his brother Balarāma. Thus all the questions and requests are related to Kṛṣṇa, who is the source of the various manifestations of the Supreme Deity. Further by asking a separate question about the biography of Kṛṣṇa, the sages indicate that there is a distinction between the descent of Kṛṣṇa and the other descents. The distinction, as we see in Sūta's reply, is that Kṛṣṇa is the perfect manifestation and revelation of Bhagavān, the Supreme Deity: [13] "This inquiry refers to Kṛṣṇa by whom the self is purified. That certainly is the highest religious duty of men from which follows devotion to Adhokṣaja."[14]

A little later Sūta uses the Hindu concept of the three forms of the Deity (*trimūrti*) to subordinate the god Hari-Viṣṇu to Kṛṣṇa Vāsudeva : "The one Supreme Person is joined to the

10. I.1.12 : sūta jānāsi bhadraṃ te bhagavānsātvatāṃpatiḥ/devakyāṃ vasudevasya jāto yasya cikīrṣayā//

11. I.1.17 : tasya karmānyudārāṇi parigītāni sūribhiḥ/ brūhi naḥ śraddadhānānāṃ līlayā dadhataḥ kalāḥ/

12. I.1.18 : athākhyāhi harerdhīmannavatārakathāḥ śubhāḥ / līlā vidadhataḥ svairamiśvarasyātmamāyayā//

13. This is not clear to some scholars, cf. David R. Kinsley, *The Sword and the Flute: Kālī and Kṛṣṇa, Dark Visions of the Terrible and the Sublime in Hindu Mythology* (Berkeley: University of California Press, 1975), p. 67, n. 19.

14. I.2.5b-6a : yatkṛtaḥ kṛṣṇasaṃpraśno yenātmā suprasīdati// sa vai puṃsāṃ paro dharmo yato bhaktiradhokṣaje/

qualities of primal nature, being, action, and inertia. He accepts for the maintenance, creation, and destruction of the universe the forms of Hari (= Viṣṇu), Viriñci (= Brahmā), and Hara (= Śiva). The supreme good for men is derived from the body of being (*sattva* = Viṣṇu)."[15] In spite of Viṣṇu's former preeminence, he is here treated as a manifestation of Bhagavān, whom Sūta has shown to be Kṛṣṇa. Sūta says that the Vedas ultimately imply Vāsudeva. The sacrifices aim at him. The disciplines of Yoga lead to him. The rituals culminate in him. All wisdom is summed up in him. All penance is done for him. All virtue is for the purpose of realizing him and all destinies converge on Vāsudeva[16] Viṣṇu is identified merely with the quality of being (*sattva*), but Kṛṣṇa-Vāsudeva is Bhagavān himself beyond the qualities. Finally all the other manifestations are his subordinates: "These are parts and portions of the Person but Kṛṣṇa is indeed Bhagavān himself."[17]

Bhagavān Kṛṣṇa

We have thus seen that one of the chief themes of the *Bhāgavata* is that Kṛṣṇa is the primary bearer of the title 'Bhagavan', that he is the Supreme Being. This identification can be seen in the many passages where the *Bhāgavata* identifies Kṛṣṇa with Viṣṇu-Nārāyaṇa. Its approach is to show that Kṛṣṇa is Viṣṇu's equal or his superior, thereby replacing him as the Highest identity of God. In canto ten Arjuna and Kṛṣṇa Journey to the highest heaven of Viṣṇu, searching for the lost sons of a Brahman. There they behold the Supreme Person, who pervades everything with his infinite powers, resting on the serpent Śeṣa. Kṛṣṇa "bowed to infinite Acyuta, who was himself." Arjuna was awestruck at the sight and bowed also. The Highest Person, Viṣṇu, addresses the two of them : "You are the sages Nara and Nārāyaṇa."[18] Here Kṛṣṇa bows to himself in

15. I.2.23 : sattvaṃ rajastama iti prakṛterguṇāstairyuktaḥ paraḥ puruṣa eka ihāsya dhatte/ sthityādaye hariviriñcihareti saṃjñāḥ śreyāṃsi tatra khalu sattvatanornṛṇāṃ syuḥ//

16. Cf. I.2.28-29.

17. I.3.28a : ete cāṃśakalāḥ puṃsaḥ kṛṣṇastu bhagavānsvayam/

18. X.89.5a, 60a :... vavanda ātmānamanantamacyuto... pūrṇakāmāvapi yuvāṃ naranārāyaṇāvṛṣī/

the form of Viṣṇu, the former preeminent Deity, and is called Nārāyaṇa by that form. Also it is indicated that Arjuna too is a manifestation of Kṛṣṇa. The two set an example to the whole world. Arjuna, "seeing the realm of Viṣṇu was much astonished. He realized that what is human in men is due to the grace of Kṛṣṇa."[19] He now understands that the two, Viṣṇu and Kṛṣṇa, are identical and that Viṣṇu has adored his companion, giving him preeminence. The two are one, Viṣṇu displaying his glory in heaven and Kṛṣṇa sporting on earth for the sake of virtue.

In canto twelve there is a Tantric meditation, presumably derived from a Pāñcarātra source. Śaunaka asks Sūta how those who follow the Tantras meditate on Viṣṇu. In reply Sūta describes Bhagavān Viṣṇu as the sun-god who manifests himself in the forms (*vyūha*) of Vāsudeva, Saṃkarṣaṇa, Pradyumna, and Aniruddha. In conclusion, Sūta addresses Viṣṇu in terms appropriate for Kṛṣṇa, identifying the two. He calls Viṣṇu the 'jewel of the Vṛṣṇis,' "Govinda, whose prowess is celebrated in song by the cowherd girls of Vraja."[20] Thus Viṣṇu is praised in terms of his divine splendor and then identified with Kṛṣṇa, who fights alongside of Arjuna and who is the beloved of the cowherd girls. The *Bhāgavata* is describing Viṣṇu in terms of Kṛṣṇa rather than vice versa.

Similarly in canto eleven Kṛṣṇa recommends to Uddhava a yogic meditation in which he is to visualize within himself the beautiful form of Kṛṣṇa, described in terms formerly used to describe Viṣṇu. Kṛṣṇa is to be conceived as having a symetrical form with a handsome face, four arms, a graceful neck and bright smiles. He is wearing the brilliant, alligator-shaped earrings of Viṣṇu: the conch, discus, mace, lotus, and the Kaustubha gem. Kṛṣṇa tells Uddhava to come to him through his Viṣṇu-form and "thus with his mind established in me, he will see me in himself and himself merged in me, the Self of all, just as light merges with light."[21] Thus the form of Viṣṇu is no

19. X.88.63 :...niśāmya vaiṣṇavaṃ dhāma pārthaḥ paramavismitaḥ/ yatkiṃcitpauruṣaṃ puṃsāṃ mene kṛṣṇānukampitam//

20. XII.11.25b: govinda gopavanitāvrajabhṛtyagīta...//

21. XI.14.45: evaṃ samāhitamatirmāmevātmānamātmani/ vicaṣṭe mayi sarvātman jyotirjyotiṣi saṃyutam//

longer that of the Supreme God but a means for Uddhava to realize his own non-dua lity with Kṛṣṇa, the Supreme Deity. While there are other passages in the *Bhāgavata* relating to Viṣṇu, some of which do not explicitly subordinate him to Kṛṣṇa, the general import of the work subordinates Viṣṇu to Kṛṣṇa. Nowhere is this more clearly seen than in the *Bhāgavata*'s treatment of the divine manifestations among men (*avatāra*).

Manifestations of the Divine: The Avatāra

The theory of the divine manifestations (*avatāra*) of Viṣṇu among men has been traced to the amalgamation of the deities Viṣṇu-Nārāyaṇa with Vāsudeva-Kṛṣṇa, the latter being understood as an incarnation of the former.[22] When it refers to the divine manifestations, the *Bhāgavata* several times alludes to this *Ṛgveda* passage : "Who can exhaust the powers of Viṣṇu ? Not even one capable of counting the particles of dust on the earth can do it."[23] Thus in canto eleven it says that "he who seeks to count the infinite qualities of the infinite has the mind of a child; it is easier to count the particles of dust on the earth in time but never the excellences of the Lord—the resort of all powers."[24] Relying on his infinite powers, Bhagavān expands himself in ways quite beyond the capacity of men to understand. The importance of these manifestations (*avatāra*) in Vaiṣṇavism, and expecially in the *Bhāgavata*, can hardly be stressed enough. The *Purāṇa*, as we have seen, begins with the questions of the sages about Kṛṣṇa's manifestations and it also concludes on this note. Thus in canto twelve Sūta tells the sages: "Thus I have answered, O best of the twice-born, what you asked about the sports, manifestations, and activities which have been related here in all their details."[25]

22. Jaiswal, *The Origin and Development of Vaiṣṇavism*, p. 118.

13. *ṚV Veda* I.154.1a : viṣṇor nu kaṃ vīryāṇi pra vocaṃ yaḥ pārthivāni vimame rajāṃsi/ Translation by Bhaṭṭācārya, *The Philosophy of the Śrīmad-Bhāgavata*, I, 174.

24. XI.4.2 : yo vā anantasya guṇānanantānanukramiṣyansa tu bālabuddhiḥ/ rajāṃsi bhūmergaṇayetkathaṃcitkālena naivākhilaśaktidhāmnaḥ//

25. XII.12.45 : iti coktaṃ dvijaśreṣthā yatpṛṣto'hamihāsmi vaḥ/ līlāvatārakarmāṇi kīrtitānīha sarvaśaḥ//

The word *avatāra* is itself rather late in the history of Vaiṣṇavism. It does not occur in the *Bhagavad Gītā* nor in the *Nārāyaṇiya* of the *Mahābhārata* nor in the *Harivaṃśa*, where such words as *janman*, *sambhava*, *sṛjana*, and *pradurbhāva* are employed.[26] The early tendency seems to have been to subordinate different deities in different localities to Viṣṇu by recognizing them as earthly manifestations of the Supreme Deity. The word *avatāra* introduces a note of systematization into the *Purāṇas*. It "implies the intrinsic superiority of the principle deity Nārāyaṇa-Viṣṇu who does an act of condescension by incarnating himself in a particular form..."[27] The original nucleus of divine manifestations was : the boar (*varāha*), the man-lion (*narasiṃha*), the dwarf (*vāmana*), and the Man who is Kṛṣṇa (*mānuṣa*), to which were later added Rāma Bhārgava and Rāma Daśaratha and then the goose (*haṃsa*), Hayagrīva, etc.[28] The number of ten manifestations was fixed soon after the *Mahābhārata*, but the names vary with the particular text, not achieving standardization before the eighth century A.D.

The *Bhāgavata* does not mention the conventional list of ten manifestations. However, lists of manifestations are mentioned in six places in the text: (1) I.3.28 where twenty-two manifestations are listed; (2) II.7.1 where twenty-four are listed; (3) VII.9.38 where seven are mentioned; (4) X.2.4 where in a celebration of the conception of Kṛṣṇa eight manifestations are mentioned; (5) X.40.17-20 where fourteen manifestations, including the four presiding manifestations (*vyūha*) are listed; and (6) XI.4.18-23 where twenty-one are listed. The *Bhāgavata*, in accord with its teaching of non-dualism, usually associates the manifestations of the Deity among men with the creation of the universe. "The widest concept of Incarnation," as S. Bhaṭṭācārya comments, "envisaged by the *Bhāgavata* here, apparently embraces all expressions of Bhagavān—immanent and transcendent, sentient and insentient—all integrated by the law of Divine Sport into the grand unity of Bhagavān."[29]

26. Jaiswal, *The Origin and Development of Vaiṣṇavism*, p. 120.
27. *Ibid.*
28. Cf. *Mahābhārata* XII.337.36.
29. Bhaṭṭācārya, *The Philosophy of the Śrīmad-Bhāgavata* I, 176.

The *avatāra*, however, is a particular immanent form of the Supreme Deity within his non-duality, the transcendent becoming immanent within the phenomenal which is ultimately not other than the Deity.

The descents of the Lord are infinite in number. As Sūta says in canto one: "Just as thousands of streams flow from an inexhaustible lake, so from the storehouse of the pure being (*sattva*) flow innumerable manifestations (*avatāra*) of Hari."[30] The sages, the Manus, the gods, those who are powerful are all rays of Hari. Again in canto ten Kṛṣṇa says that his own "births, actions, and names number in the thousands, and cannot be counted by me because they are infinite."[31] Recalling the *Ṛg Veda*, Kṛṣṇa says that "someone in the past might have been able to count the particles of dust on the earth through many lives, but one could never count my qualities, actions, names, and births."[32] The births (*janman*) and the manifestations (*avatāra*) of the Divine are infinite in number and manifest the infinite power of Bhagavān to express himself, yet they, in spite of their non-duality with him, are but partial expressions of his infinite power.

The *Bhāgavata* in different places in the text classifies the divine manifestations differently. Thus the first canto says that the manifestations are "parts (*aṃśa*) and portions (*kala*) of the Person."[33] In addition to the part and portion manifestions there is a hybrid of the two types (*aṃśa-kala*). The part manifestations (*aṃśa*) are parts of God's omniscience and omnipotence which enter the phenomenal process on the behalf of men. For instance in canto eight Śuka says that, when Aditi received the gift of giving birth to a manifestation of Hari, she waited upon her husband Kaśyapa. Kaśyapa meditated and saw "a part (*aṁśa*) of Hari entering his self. He then placed his seed long conserved by

30. I.3.26 : avatārā hyasaṃkhyeyā hareḥ sattvanidherdvijāḥ/yathā'vidāsinaḥ kulyāḥ sarasaḥ syuḥ sahasraśaḥ//

31. X.51.37 : janmakarmābhidhānāni santi me'ṅga sahasraśaḥ/ na śakhyante'nusaṃkhyātumanantatvānmayāpi hi//

32. X.51.38: kvacidrajāṃsi vimame pārthivānyurujanmabhiḥ/ guṇakarmābhidhānāni na me janmāni karhicit// Cf. *Ṛg Veda* I.154.1a.

33. I.3.18a : ete cāṃśakalāh puṃsāḥ.../

penance in Aditi."[34] In this manner Bhagavān entered the human race in the form of Kapila, who was thus a part manifestation of Bhagavān. The part manifestation can take place by Bhagavān possessing a person in a unique way; it is a displacement of normal human processes by God. On the other hand, the portion manifestations (*kala*) are God-filled persons. In canto one the gods are described as portion manifestations.[35] Among humans Vyāsa, Gaya, Datta, and Kumāra are portion manifestations of Hari, persons who are filled with God. The hybrid type of manifestation (*aṃśa-kala*) is part man part God. For example the *avatāra* Ṛṣabha is of this type. In the fifth canto Bhagavān decides to "descend through Nābhi (Ṛṣabha's father) exhibiting a part-portion of my own."[36] This type of classification is, however, only used sparingly in the *Bhāgavata*, though it would find currency in the systematics of those who hold the *Bhāgavata* as authoritative.

The Cosmic Manifestations (*guṇāvatāra*)

Since creation in the *Bhāgavata* has the purpose of forming a realm for the playful sports of Bhagavān, Bhagavān manifests himself to superintend the different phases of his creation by means of the cosmic manifestations (*guṇāvatāra*). In the process of creation from the unmanifest primal nature (*avyakta prakṛti*) there emerge the three constituent qualities (*guṇa*), the pure being (*sattva*), action (*rajas*), and inertia (*tamas*). In canto one Sūta describes the qualities which are assumed for the maintenance, creation, and destruction of the universe. The Highest Person accepts for this purpose the forms of Hari, Viriñci, and Hara.[37] Here the name of Bhagavān's manifestation varies according to the mission of the particular quality. Again in canto three Vidura asks Maitreya to "kindly recount the glorious activities of him who is the abode of Śrī and of him who creates,

34. VIII.17.23ab : praviṣṭamātmani harerаṃśaṃ hyavitathekṣaṇaḥ/ so'dityāṃ vīryamādhatta tapasā cirasaṃbhṛtam/Cf. IV.14.22; IX.22.21; X.15.9; X.4.17.

35. Cf. I.3.27-

36. V.3.18: tata āgnīdhrīyeṃ'śakalayā'vatariṣyāmyātmatulyamanupalabhamānaḥ//

37. Cf. I.2.23.

destroys and maintains the universe through the cosmic manifestations."[38] The doctrine of the cosmic manifestations or the *trimūrti* of Bhagavān coordinates each of the three great gods of Hinduism with the one quality to which he is suited and thereby subordinates them to the Supreme Deity, Bhagavān Kṛṣṇa, who is ultimately beyond the process of creation while these gods are not. Thus Viṣṇu is the pure being (*sattva*), Brahmā is action (*rajas*), and Śiva is inertia (*tamas*). In canto four the *Bhāgavata* emphasizes the unity and inter-relatedness of the cosmic manifestations: "O Brahman, he who sees no difference between the three of us who are essentially one and the selves of all creatures attains peace."[39] The cosmic manifestations are thus the mediators of reality from the absolute reality of Bhagavān to the relative reality of each individual being. Actually they are identical with Bhagavān and an expression of his non-duality. The equation of Viṣṇu, however, with the quality of pure being (*sattva*) is in accord with his preeminence, in the minds of Vaiṣṇavas, over Brahmā and especially over Śiva. The *Bhāgavata* in the first canto recalls that formerly Viṣṇu was worshipped as the preeminent God: "Formerly sages worshipped Bhagavān Adhokṣaja, who is pure being."[40] But in the Kali age now that Kṛṣṇa has appeared and made himself known the true identity of Bhagavān as Kṛṣṇa, and the subordination of Viṣṇu to him, is apparent.

The Presiding Manifestations (*vyūha*)

The former supremacy of Viṣṇu and his current subordination to Kṛṣṇa is further illustrated in the *Bhāgavata*'s absorption of the Pāñcarātra doctrine of the presiding manifestations (*vyūha*) within its teaching about the *avatāras*. There is a definite down-grading of the role and place of the presiding manifestations in the *Bhāgavata* in contrast to the Pāñcarātra literature. They

38. III.7.28 : guṇāvatārairviśvasya sargasthityapyayāśrayam/ sṛjataḥ śrīnivāsasya vyācakṣvodāravikramam//

39. IV.7.54 : trayāṇāmekabhāvānāṃ yo na paśyati vai bhidām/ sarva-bhūtātmanāṃ brahmansa śāntimadhigacchati//

40. I.2.25 : bhejire munayo'thāgre bhagavantamadhokṣajam/sattvaṃ viśuddhaṃ...//

play only a peripheral role in the *Bhāgavata*'s teaching, being used chiefly as titles and epithets. However, three passages give some emphasis to the presiding deities. In canto four the presiding manifestations are given a cosmological function:

> Praise to Vasudeva who has a lotus sprung from his navel, who is the Self of the senses and the subtle elements, who is tranquil, immutable, and self-luminous.
>
> Praise to Saṃkarṣaṇa, who is subtle, infinite, who brings the end (of the universe), and to Pradyumna who is the highest knowledge of the universe in the interior Self.
>
> Praise, praise to Aniruddha, the self of the mind, presiding over the senses.[41]

There is a Vedāntic cosmological teaching here, which contrasts with the Sāṃkhya of the *Bhāgavata*'s usual teaching. However, as the following two passages show, consistency is lacking in the *Bhāgavata*'s use of the presiding manifestation doctrine. In canto three Kapila, in the midst of his teaching about Sāṃkhya, connects that doctrine with the doctrine of the presiding manifestations (*vyūha*). Kapila correlates the cosmic intelligence (*citta*) or great principle (*mahat*) with the presiding manifestation Vāsudeva. The threefold ego (*ahaṃkāra*) is connected with Saṃkarṣaṇa and mind (*manas*) is joined to Aniruddha.[42] Strangely there is no mention here of the third presiding manifestation, Pradyumna, and only Aniruddha can be correlated with the functions described in the previous passage. Finally in canto twelve there is a description of Tantric teaching, which is closely related to the Pāñcarātra. Here the four presiding manifestations are compared to the four states of the empirical ego: the waking state, dreaming, deep sleep, and the fourth state or self-realization. Each presiding manifestation presides over a state, Vāsudeva over the fourth state, Saṃkarṣaṇa over deep sleep, Pradyumna over dreaming, and Aniruddha over the waking

41. IV.24.34-36a namaḥ paṅkajanābhāya bhūtasūkṣmendriyātmane/ vāsudevāya śāntāya kūṭasthāya svarociṣe// saṃkarṣaṇāya sūkṣmāya durantāyāntakāya ca/ namo viśvaprabodhāya pradyumnāyāntarātmane// namo-namo'niruddhāya hṛṣīkeśendriyātmane/

42. Cf. III.26.21,95,28.

state.[43] There is no mention in canto twelve of any cosmological significance for the presiding manifestations. The inconsistency of these three passages about the presiding manifestations (*vyūha*) can be seen in the following chart:

IV.24.34-36	III.26.21-28	XII.11.21-23
Vāsudeva-transcendent	-intelligence	-self realization
Saṃkarṣaṇa-destroyer	-ego	-deep sleep
Pradyumna-cosmic knowledge		-dreaming
Aniruddha-over the senses	-mind	-waking state

Thus we can see that the presiding manifestation (*vyūha*) doctrine so elaborately developed in the *Pāñcarātra Saṃhitās* remains peripheral to the theology of the *Bhāgavata*. In so far as it is used at all, it is inconsistent. The fact that it has been included in the *Bhāgavata* is probably due to the eclectic tendency of the *Purāṇa*.

The Play Manifestations (*līlāvatāra*)

What is usually understood by the term *avatāra* or manifestation is described in the *Bhāgavata* as the play manifestation (*līlāvatāra*) of Bhagavān in the world of humans. The play manifestations are the main subjects of the *Bhāgavata*'s narrations. In canto one Sūta says that Bhagavān creates the different worlds and appears for sport (*līlāvatāra*) in the guise of gods, human beings, and animals. His purpose is to protect by means of his quality of pure being (*sattva*).[44] In canto two hearing about this kind of manifestation "dries up the impurities of the ears and is pleasing to the heart and to be relished."[45] The cosmic manifestations are concerned with the universe and the presiding manifestations with the states of a person's mind; the play manifestation (*līlāvatāra*) is Bhagavān come to dwell among men in his different forms—man, animal, fish, etc. Bhagavān's main purpose is the protection of the universe and of his creatures. As Prahlāda says in canto seven: "In this way you

43. Cf. XII.11.21-23.
44. Cf. I.2.34.
45. II.6.45b : āpīyatāṃ karṇakaṣāyaśoṣānanukamiṣye ta imānsupeśān//

protect the world and kill the people's enemies through the manifestations as man, beasts, sages, gods, and the fish, O Great Person; you maintain the religious status (*dharma*) prevalent in each age."[46] Bhagavān also comes to earth "in deference to the wishes of the devotees."[47] The devotees would be bereft of their innermost self without Bhagavān. He assumes a human form in order to win the confidence of men and to show them the glory and splendor of the Divine Being. While one purpose of a manifestation is to rid the earth of demons, "the human manifestation of the Lord is really for the instruction of mankind."[48] Because he comes to teach men how to live and to follow the highest religious teaching, the Lord performs actions which are paradigmatic or examples which reveal the meaning of life. For instance, the Lord, who is satisfied in his Self, sported in the form of Rāma with Sītā. The purpose of this manifestatlon is to instruct men in the hidden inner meaning of life.[49] The intensity of the Lord's separation from her is to teach men what happens when they are attached to worldly pleasures. In addition it illustrates the importance of woman's fidelity.

Another motive for Bhagavān's manifestations is to show men the way to liberation: "O Lord, I resort to you who have enkindled the lamp of your glory by means of your play manifestations. Those selves wander in the cycle of death and rebirth and do not know how to achieve final liberation from the body, which is the source of evil."[50] Thus Kṛṣṇa is the greatest source of inspiration because he attracted the people with his personality which towered over all others. He taught the people with his words and freed them from the effects of their actions. He retired to his abode because now the singing of his fame and spreading of his renown suppresses the darkness.

46. VII.9.38 : ittham nṛtiryagṛṣidevaśpaṣāvatārairlokānvibhāvayasi hamsi jagatpratīpān/ dharmaṃ mahāpuruṣa pāsi yugānuvṛttam channaḥ...//

47. X.59.25b : . . . bhaktecchā...//

48. V.19.5a: martyāvatārastviha martyaśikṣaṇaṃ. . .kevalaṃ vibhoḥ/

49. Cf. V.19.5b.

50. X.70.39 : jīvasya yaḥ saṃsarato vimokṣaṇaṃ na jānato' narthavahāccharīrataḥ/ līlāvatāraiḥ svayaśaḥ pradīpakaṃ prājvālayattvā tamahaṃ prapadye//

While the *Bhāgavata* includes Kṛṣṇa in its lists of the manifestations, it also identifies him in a special way with the Bhagavān who so manifests himself. In canto ten the *Bhāgavata* says that it is Kṛṣṇa who manifests himself through the manifestations (*avatāra*) in order "to relieve the burden of earth . . .having descended in the form of a fish, horse, tortoise, man-lion, bear, goose, king, Brahman, and God."[51] The *Bhāgavata* also describes Kṛṣṇa as a part manifestation (*aṃśa*) when it says that Bhagavān entered the mind of Kṛṣṇa's father "with all his divine potencies constituting part manifestations of his being."[52] In another place Kṛṣṇa is described as a portion manifestation (*kala*): "You have appeared on earth by your portion manifestations for protecting religion (*dharma*)."[53] It has been seen that all manifestations are consubstantial with Bhagavān, though they may only partially manifest his being. This accords with *Bhāgavata*'s non-dualism. The Kṛṣṇa manifestation, however, stands out. The original questions of the sages singled out the Kṛṣṇa story and Sūta's reply to those questions affirmed Kṛṣṇa's singular identification with Bhagavān. While listing Kṛṣṇa among the twenty-four manifestations (*aṃśakala*) of Bhagavān through the Person (*puruṣa*), Sūta definitively states: "Kṛṣṇa indeed is Bhagavān himself."[54] Śrīdhara in his comment on this text emphasizes Kṛṣṇa's uniqueness: Kṛṣṇa is perfect (*pūrṇa*) because all potencies are seen to be in full swing in this Descent. Though the other Descents like the Fish and the Tortoise do emanate from the same reality, i.e. Bhagavān, yet all the potencies are not brought into play in the case of the other Descents."[55] Thus the same context describes Kṛṣṇa as both part (*aṃśa*) and full (*pūrṇa*) manifestation. Yet the meaning is clear. The *Bhāgavata* is emphatic in describing Kṛṣṇa as Bhagavān, and in its total

51. X.2.40a : matsyāśvakacchapanṛsiṃhavarāhahaṃsarājanyavipravibudheṣu kṛtāvatāraḥ /

52. X.2.16b : āviveśāṃśabhāgena mana ānakadundubheḥ//

53. X.89.59 : ..bhuvi dharmaguptaye/ kalāvatīrṇāvavaner,..//

54. I.3.28a :...kṛṣṇastu bhagavānsvayam/

55. *Bhāgavata Bhāvārtha Dīpika* on I.3.28. quoted in Bhaṭṭācārya, *The Philosophy of the Śrīmad-Bhāgavata*, I, 88 : tatra matsyādīnāṃ avatāratvena sarvajñatve sarvaśaktimattve'pi yathopayogaṃ eva jñānakriyāśakyāviṣkaraṇam...kṛṣṇas tu sākṣāt bhagavān nārāyaṇa eva āviṣkṛtasarvaśaktimattvāt/

import subordinates every other manifestation to that of Kṛṣṇa. Perhaps as Śrīdhara suggests, the *Bhagavata* allows the ascription of a partial character to the Kṛṣṇa manifestation as a concession to the partial nature of the perception of the observer.

Kṛṣṇa is the complete (*pūrṇa*) manifestation. The first nine cantos described his earlier manifestations, the tenth deals with his life and activities exclusively. They first nine cantos form a prologue, teaching indeed about Bhagavān Kṛṣṇa, but only in order to show forth his full glory and splendor in the tenth canto. The *Bhāgavata* never describes Kṛṣṇa as merely a man. He is always the Supreme Deity, but all the same definitely a man. Thus at his birth to Devakī, Vasudeva, his father, saw an extraordinary sight. Kṛṣṇa was beheld in all his divine nature with four arms holding the accouterments of Viṣṇu, the conch, mace, and discus. He was wearing the Śrīvatsa curl and the Kaustubha gem.[56] Thus his birth as a human is also a divine epiphany. Whenever he hid his divine nature, an exquisite human beauty was beheld by his friends in Vṛndāvana: "Kṛṣṇa of dark blue complexion, wearing a golden silk garment, dressed like an actor with a wreath of forest flowers, peacock feathers and leaves, beautified with mineral paints, who rested one hand on the shoulders of his companions and dangled a lotus in the other, with lilies gracing his ears, and curls of hair hanging on his cheeks, a smile on his face."[57]

Such is the perfect young boy in his rustic garb that the cowherd girls beheld and yearned for. The place of his boyhood becomes diaphanous with his transcendence. The *Bhāgavata*'s description of Vṛndāvana oscillates between heaven and earth. It is as much a matter of Kṛṣṇa bringing a piece of earth up to heaven as of Kṛṣṇa bringing heaven down to earth. Vṛndāvana by Kṛṣṇa's presence becomes a paradigm of heavenly existence. Thus Brahmā exclaims that his greatest fortune would be to be born "in Gokula bathing in the dust of its inhabitants' feet, for

56. Cf. X.3.9-10.

57. X.23.22 : śyāmaṃ hiraṇyaparidhiṃ vanamālyabarhadhātupravālanaṭaveṣamanuvratāṃse/ vinyastahastamitareṇa dhunānamabjaṃ karṇotpalālakakapolamukhābjahāsam//

their entire life is completely Bhagavān Mukunda; indeed even now the Vedas seek the dust of his feet."[58]

This Kṛṣṇa is the Self of all living beings. For the good of the world and its inhabitants he descends by means of his creative energy in the form of a human. If one knows him, then he knows everything that can be known. Everything becomes a manifestation of him, who is the cause of everything.[59] The *Bhāgavata* repeatedly affirms the non-dual meaning of the Kṛṣṇa manifestation. He dwells in the hearts of all his created beings the way fire resides in wood. Everyone is equally dear to him; he is the same to all. He has no mother, father, wife, nor children; no action is his, "but for the sake of sport and for the protection of the righteous he is born in the good, bad, and mixed (kinds of species)."[60]

Although he is beyond the qualities, he assumes the qualities for the sake of men. "Nothing which is seen or heard, which has happened, is now, or is to come, nothing which is immobile or mobile, large or small, should be named apart from Acyuta; for only he is everything and real."[61]

Here Kṛṣṇa is clearly identified as the Supreme Being. He assumes the titles of Viṣṇu, who becomes a mere cosmic manifestation. As the complete (*pūrṇa*) manifestation of the Supreme Being he has entered his own creation for the purpose of play (*līlā*). Kṛṣṇa, when he sported among the cowherd girls, perfectly manifested the being and splendor of the Supreme Deity and he perfectly revealed his ultimate purpose and his divine nature. He is one, non-dual, above all qualities, yet these qualities are contained in him. The *Bhāgavata* describes Kṛṣṇa from a difference-in-identity (*bhedābheda*) viewpoint. He is non-dual with qualifications (*saviśeṣādvaita*). Without grounding

58. X.14.34 : tadbhūribhāgyamihajanma kimapyaṭavyāṃ yadgokule'pi katamāṅghrirajobhiṣekam/ yajjīvitaṃ tu nikhilaṃ bhagavānmukundastvadyāpi yatpadarajaḥ śrutimṛgyameva//

59. Cf. X.14.55-57.

60. X.46.39 : na cāsya karma vā loke sadasanmiśrayoniṣu/ krīḍārthaḥ so'pi sādhūnāṃ paritrāṇāya kalpate//

61. X.46.43 : draṣṭaṃ śrutaṃ bhūtabhavadbhaviṣyat sthāsnuścariṣṇurmahadalpakaṃ ca/vinā'cyutādvastu tarāṃ na vācyaṃ sa eva sarvaṃ paramārthabhūtaḥ//

this position philosophically to the extent the later Vaiṣṇava *ācāryas* would attempt, the *Bhāgavata*'s redactor, as a Bhāgavata devoted to Kṛṣṇa, appealed to the non-dualism of Vaiṣṇavism and Vedānta, within a Sāṃkhya framework, since Kṛṣṇa was really active and involved in his creation. In the next chapter we shall describe how these apparently contradictory assertions are warranted by an intense devotion to Kṛṣṇa, the Supreme Deity.

Chapter V

DEVOTION : THE REALITY OF BHAGAVĀN

The Forms of Devotion

The *Bhāgavata* has been described as "a working paper for the *bhakti* movment, not a clearly formulated and rigidly edited document."[1] It reflects the long history, development, and heritage of the Vaiṣṇava devotional movement, being separated from the *Bhagavad Gītā* by as much as a millennium. It also reflects the new tumultuous ferment of Vaiṣṇavism's transition to Kṛṣṇaism. The *Bhāgavata* is a quite different document from the *Bhagavad Gītā* because the devotion it preaches incorporates the sweetness (*mādhurya*) aspect of Kṛṣṇa's character as a romantic lover, which at the time of the *Bhāgavata* was displacing the powerful (*aiśvarya*) aspect of his character as a warrior prince. The present chapter will treat the conservative *aiśvarya* trend of devotion as a meditative process, which was derived from the *Bhagavad Gītā*, while the next chapter will consider the *Bhāgavata*'s innovative devotion as emotional and loving ecstasy, which was derived from sources like the Āḷvārs.

Devotion is closely linked with the idea of a personal God, who bestows divine grace on his devotee who, in his turn, responds with devotional service to the Deity. Although hints of devotion are found in the *Upaniṣads*, its first clear exposition is found in the *Bhagavad Gītā*.[2] Here it is already bound up with the non-dualism of the *Upaniṣads*. The highest being, Kṛṣṇa, even though he contains the entire cosmos and is inconceivable, reveals himself in a physical, adorable form. The

1. Hopkins, "Vaishṇava Bhakti Movement in the *Bhāgavāta Purāṇa*," p. 164.
2. Jaiswal, *Origin and Development of Vaiṣṇavism*, p. 112.

devotee, by the grace of Kṛṣṇa, forms a feeling of intimacy with him, like that between friends, or between father and son, or lover and beloved. Arjuna says: "Therefore bowing down and prostrating my body before you, Adorable Lord, I seek your grace; you, O God, should bear with me as a father to his son, as a friend to his friend, as a lover to his beloved."[3] There is no tinge here of emotional love of the devotee for the Lord since the *Gītā* is always conscious of the transcendence of the Deity.[4] Devotion is accompanied by intellectual conviction and faith: "The great-souled, O Pārtha, who abide in the divine nature, knowing me as the imperishable source of all beings, worship me with an undistracted mind."[5] Thus devotion arises out of faith in the Deity: "Endowed with that faith, he seeks the worship of such a one and from him he obtain his desires. the benefits being decreed by me alone."[6] Erotic mystical devotion is practically totally absent; devotion is for the learned and the wise, who can follow the path of knowledge. The emphasis is on a quiet, simple faith which worships Kṛṣṇa the warrior prince.

The *Bhāgavata* makes extensive use of the type of devotion found in the *Gītā*, and especially develops its links to the path of knowledge and to Yoga. As in the *Gītā*, devotion in the *Bhāgavata* is often called a discipline (*yoga*), a means to final liberation (*sādhana*). In canto one the discipline of devotion (*bhaktiyoga*) is described as the motive for Vyāsa's composing the *Bhāgavata*. The context links devotion to the practice of meditation on the Supreme Person: "In his sinless mind perfectly concentrated by means of the discipline of devotion, he saw the Primal Person and his creative energy, which depends

3. *Bhagavad Gītā* XI.44 : tasmātpraṇamya praṇidhāya kāyaṃ prasādaye tvāmahamīśamīḍyam/ piteva putrasya sakheva sakhyuḥ priyaḥ priyāyārhasi deva soḍhum// Translated by Sarvepalli Radhakrishnan in Sarvepalli Radhakrishnan and Charles A. Moore, *A Sourcebook in Indian Philosophy* (Princeton : Princeton University Press, 1957), p. 142.

4. Ch. Vaudeville, "Evolution of Love-Symbolism in Bhagavatism," *Journal of the American Oriental Society*, LXXXII (March 1962), 33.

5. *Bhāgavad Gītā* IX.13 : mahātmānastu māṃ pārtha daivīṃ prakṛtimāśritāḥ/ bhajantyananyamanaso jñātvā bhūtādimavyayam// p. 133.

6. *Bhagavad Gītā* VII.22 : sa tayā śraddhayā yuktastasyārādhanamīhate/ labhate ca tataḥ kāmānmayaiva vihitānhi tān// p. 128.

on him."[7] The individual self deluded by the creative energy indentifies itself with the sphere of the three qualities, although the three qualities, do not touch Bhagavān's essence. This identification brings evil consequences. Since most men are unaware that the discipline of devotion to Kṛṣṇa counteracts those evil consequences, Vyāsa composed the *Bhāgavata* so that "by listening to this, devotion to Kṛṣṇa the Supreme Person, arises, which dispels a person's fear, delusion, and sorrow."[8] Devotion overcomes this bondage by surpassing the realm of Bhagavān's creative energy and centers its attention exclusively on Kṛṣṇa. Merely listening to his exploits stirs up the sentiment of devotion. Devotion is the goal of devotion as well as the means. Thus Vyāsa composed the *Bhāgavata* for the common people whose ignorance will be thereby dispelled.

Devotion also takes one away from the self-concern and self-centeredness of certain types of Yoga and ritual action. It brings one to think only of Bhagavān. In canto two Śuka tells Parīkṣit : "O King, even ascetics who have turned away from abiding by commandments and prohibitions and who are beyond the realm of the qualities delight in discoursing about the qualities of Hari."[9] Every other goal, even the selfless states pursued by the ascetics, is put aside in order to devote oneself completely to the service of Bhagavān. In conto three Kapila tells his mother Devahūtī that the "devotees of Bhagavān delight in the service of my feet and are happily engaged in activities for my sake. With deep interest and affection, they enjoy describing to one another my human exploits. They never desire to become one self with me."[10] Here the highest goal of the non-dualist sages which is absorption (*ekātmatām*) is superceded by devotion, although as we shall see, the *Bhāgavata* is not consistent on this point. Devotion because it keeps Bhagavān always in view transcends liberation (*mukti*).

7. I.7.4 : bhaktiyogena manasi samyak praṇihite'male/ apaśyatpuruṣaṃ pūrvaṃ māyāṃ ca tadupāśrayām//

8. I.7.7 : yasyāṃ vai śrūyamāṇāyāṃ kṛṣṇe paramapūruṣe/ bhaktirutpadyate puṃsaḥ śokamohabhayāpahā//

9. II.1.7 : prāyeṇa munayo rājannivṛttā vidhiṣedhataḥ nairguṇyasthā ramante sma guṇānukathane hareḥ//

10. III.25.34 : naikātmatāṃ me spṛhayanti kecinmatpādasevābhiratā madīhāḥ/ ye'nyonyato bhāgavatāḥ prasajjya sabhājayante mama pauruṣāṇi//

Having distinguished devotion from liberation, the *Bhāgavata* gives a definition of devotion. In canto three Kapila defines devotion twice. The first definition is in chapter twenty-three where devotion is a natural inclination of the senses, whose objects are the qualities and whose actions are in accord with Scripture, toward the quality of pure being (*sattva*) which is the quality nearest to Bhgavān.[11] This motiveless devotion is superior to final beatitude itself. It quickly dissolves the body just as the stomach consumes what is eaten. The effort to reach beatitude is imperfect since it is concerned with the self. If the hindrances present in the realm of the qualities be removed, the senses will follow their natural inclination and seek out Bhagavān. Devotion is thus the natural inclination to center one's attention upon Bhagavān, which occurs when all personal motives have been removed. Both the entanglement of the senses in the performance of the Vedic injunctions and the disentanglement of the senses from the performance of the injunctions in the search for beatitude (*siddhi*) obscure the natural end of the person which is devotional service to Bhagavān.

Another definition of devotion is given in the twenty-ninth chapter of canto three where Kapila, who is a manifestation of Bhagavān, says that "the mind incessantly flows to me, who reside in the hearts of all, by means of listening to my qualities, just as the water of the Ganges continuously moves to the ocean. This is the defining characteristic of the discipline of devotion which is without qualities and without ulterior motive; it is without cause, this uninterrupted devotion to the Supreme Person."[12] There is a natural affinity of the devotee for Bhagavān. His devotion is never interrupted because the devotee recognizes the presence of Bhagavān within his heart. This presence is in no way contaminated by the qualities of material or psychic nature. Yet the presence of Bhagavān is not exclusively interior. The prompting cause of this movement to Bhagavān is the "listening to my qualities", which suggests that

11. Cf. III.25.32-33a.

12. III.29.11-12 : madguṇaśrutimātreṇa mayi sarvaguhāśaye/ manogatiravicchinnā tathā gaṅgāmbhaso'mbudhau//lakṣaṇaṃ bhaktiyogasya nirguṇasya hyudāhṛtaṃ/ ahaitukyavyavahitā yā bhaktiḥ puruṣottame//

the entrance of Bhagavān as an *avatāra* into the sphere of the qualities is the external exemplar for the interior movement.

Just as it is not sufficient to be concerned with self-liberation, so too devotion, for the *Bhāgavata,* does not turn in on itself in an exclusive one-to-one relationship with the Lord. The devotee, who is saddened by the lack of devotion in others, lives not for himself but for others. As Śaunaka says of the king Parīkṣit that "men who are devoted to his highest praises live for the happiness, affluence, and prosperity of the world and not for themselves."[13] Thus the *Bhāgavata* on occasion gives a positive value to the world. It tells a king to be concerned for his subjects. A more profound concern is exhibited in canto seven by Prahlāda : "O Supreme, my mind is immersed in the great nectar of songs of your deeds; I am not afraid to cross the river Vaitaraṇi, which is so hard to cross; I lament only for the deluded who being averse carry on the burden of the family in hope of securing the pleasures of the creative energy's sense objects."[14] Prahlāda is not one of those ascetics who desire their own liberation and thus practice quiet meditation in solitude, uninterested in others. He does "not wish to be liberated alone."[15] So he says that there is no other refuge than Bhagavān for those who are perplexed about the meaning of life.

Devotion is both motiveless and causeless. Since devotion is the highest religious duty of men, it must be completely unsullied by any base motive or cause from any other duty. Kṛṣṇa is himself its only cause and accompanying devotion to him is knowledge and detachment. These two are subordinated to devotion. Devotion brings knowledge and knowledge brings detachment but not vice versa since devotion is causeless, springing only from the grace of Kṛṣṇa. Śaunaka in canto one expresses surprise that anyone would want to move beyond the ascetic's delight in the self (*ātmārāma*) to devotion. He remarks

13. I.4.12 : śivāya lokasya bhavāya bhūtaye ya uttamaślokaparāyaṇā janāḥ jīvanti nātmārthamasau parāśrayaṃ mumoca nirvidya kutaḥ kalevaram /

14. VII.9.43 : naivodvije para duratyayavaitaraṇyāstvadvīryagāyanamahāmṛtamagnacittaḥ/ śoce tato vimukhacetasa indriyārthamāyasukhāya bharamudvahato vimūḍhān//

15. VII.9.44b : . . . vimumukṣa eko na...//

that Śuka was "devoid of attachment to the world and indifferent to everything. Why did he, who was delighting in the self, turn to this large book."[16] To which Sūta replies that "even sages who delight in the self and are freed from the knots of ignorance practice motiveless devotion to the Wide-Strider because the qualities of Hari are so wonderful."[17] Being free from the state of bondage and free from ignorance is not the reason the sages practice devotion. Devotion is not caused by any prior state in the devotee. The devotee is attracted to Bhagavān because of his great qualities and thus leaves behind his own accomplishments, no matter how great.

In canto eleven there is a description of the devotee of Bhagavān, particularly of those qualities which make him beloved by Bhagavān. Hari (a sage) says that "he is the foremost devotee of Bhagavān who sees his own self existing in all beings as Bhagavān and sees all beings in the self which is Bhagavān."[18] The devotee sees Bhagavān present everywhere since he is part of Bhagavān and everywhere Bhagavān is, he is. He does not discriminate between creatures but is devoted to them all as forms of Bhagavān. Hari continues : "He is the foremost devotee of Bhagavān who, grasping objects with his senses, neither hates nor delights in them since he sees this world as the creative energy of Viṣṇu."[19] The universe is Viṣṇu's creation, as such the devotee does not disdain it, but because the creative energy is also the cause of delusion among men, the devotee keeps his distance and is detached from it. "He is the devotee of Bhagavān, who by remembering Hari, is not confused by the conditions of death-rebirth cycles such as birth and death affecting the body, hunger and thirst (harassing) the vital

16. I.7.9 : sa vai nivṛttiniratah sarvatropekṣako muniḥ/ kasya vā bṛhatīmetāmātmāramaḥ samabhyasat//

17. I.7.10 : ātmārāmāśca munayo nirgranthā apyurukrame/ kurvantyahaitukīṃ bhaktimitthaṃbhūtaguṇo hariḥ//

18. XI.2.45 : sarvabhūteṣu yaḥ paśyedbhagavadbhāvamātmanaḥ/ bhūtāṇi bhagavatyātmanyeṣa bhāgavatottamaḥ// Cf. *Bhagavad Gītā* VI. 30 : yo māṃ paśyati sarvatra sarvaṃ ca mayi paśyati/ tasyāhaṃ na praṇaśyāmi sa ca me na praṇaśyati// "He who sees me everywhere and sees all in me—I am not lost to him nor is he lost to me." p. 25.

19. XI.2.48 : gṛhītvāpīndriyairarthān yo na dveṣṭhi na hṛṇyati/ viṣṇormāyāmidaṃ paśyansa vai bhāgavatottamaḥ//

principle, fear (worrying) the mind, desire (exciting) the intellect and fatigue exhausting the senses."[20] In the mind of the devotee the seeds of desire and action never sprout.[21] Devotion thus removes the causes of the death-rebirth cycle (*saṃsāra*). The only refuge is Kṛṣṇa. The devotee does not identify himself with his body. He takes no pride in anything he has done or anything he is, such as his caste or stage in life (*āśrāma*). He is tranquil because all things are equal in his eyes. Indeed, Hari continues: "He is the foremost Vaiṣṇava who will not allow the memory of the Lord to be interrupted even for half a wink for gaining the sovereignty of the three worlds. Nor does he waver even for half the twinkling of the eyelid from the lotus-feet of Bhagavān which are sought by the gods and others who have never subdued the self."[22] The foremost devotee is the one whom the Lord does not leave since the two are tied together by the cord of love. For the *Bhāgavata* the quality of devotion is commensurate with the quality of the devotee's knowledge or vision of the divine Kṛṣṇa. The highest devotion is to see God's presense engulfing all his creatures. The details of that creation are not disregarded but integrated into a vision of the divine unity of Bhagavān and his creatures. Thus the devotion here described is closely akin to the way of knowledge.

The *Bhāgavata*, following the tradition of the *Bhagavad Gītā*, opens up the benefits of devotion to everyone, regardless of class, caste, sex, or race.[23] The Kirātas, Huns, Āndhras, Pulindas, Pulkasas, Ābhīras, Kaṇkas, Yavanas, Khasas, "and others are purged of their sins, even by taking refuge in those who depend on him."[24] This inclusiveness was not intended to be mere theory. Bhagavān's power is unlimited and he works through

20. XI.2.49 : dehendriyaprāṇamanodhiyāṃ yo janmāpyayakṣudbhayatarṣakṛccraiḥ/ saṃsāradharmairavimuhyamāḥ smṛtyā harerbhāgavatapradhānaḥ//

21. Cf. XI.2.50.

22. XI.2.53 : tribhuvanavibhavahetave'pyakuṇḍhasmṛtirajitātmasurādibhirvimṛgyāt/ na calati bhagavatpadāravindāllavanimiṣārdhamapi yaḥ sa vaiṣṇavāgryaḥ//

23. Cf. *Bhagavad Gītā* IX.30-32.

24. II.4.18 : kirātahūṇāndhrapulindapulkasā ābhīrakaṅkā yavanāḥ khasādayah/ ye'nye ca pāpā yadupāśrayāśrayāḥ śudhyanti. . .//

his devotees who on his behalf extend that power to other men.

The *Bhāgavata* also considers forms of devotion which are imperfect. The imperfection resides in the attitude of the devotee. Since perfect devotion comes from Bhagavān himself, it is not subject to degrees since devotion is ultimately Bhagavān's own attitude toward himself. Degrees of perfection in devotion are attributed to the individual's progress toward purity from the effects of the three qualities (*guṇa*). The mind is constituted of a mixture of the three qualities in varying degrees. Hence, the *Bhāgavata* accordingly classifies imperfect devotion into three types, devotion of pure consciousness (*sāttvika*), of action (*rājasa*), and of inertia (*tāmasa*), depending upon which quality predominates in the mind and attitude of the devotee. As Kapila tells Devahūtī in canto three: "The discipline of devotion is of many kinds according to the different paths; the objects of men differ according to their natural dispositions and qualities."[25]

The devotion of a devotee in whom inertia (*tamas*) predominates is the lowest kind: "He who becomes my devotee with the intention of doing injury or out of hypocrisy and jealously or out of anger, or with an outlook full of differences is an inertial type (*tāmasa*)."[26] The man who worships through an image, who makes distinctions between things and himself, and who seeks fame and power is of the action type (*rājasa*). The lower types of devotion put a distinction between the devotee and Bhagavān. There is still gratification in the objects of the senses and Bhagavān is treated as an object of the senses who gives gratification. This devotee is still not of one mind and heart with Bhagavān. "He who wishes to purge all karmas, or desires to dedicate them to the Supreme Lord, or worships the Lord with the simple objective of worship but entertains the idea of difference, is of the pure consciousness (*sāttvika*) type."[27] However even the pure consciousness devotee is still not pure. He

25. III.29.7 : bnaktiyogo bahuvidho mārgairbhāmini bhāvyate/ svabhāvaguṇamārgena puṃsāṃ bhāvo vibhidyate//

26. III.29.8 : abhisaṃdhāya yo hiṃsāṃ dambhaṃ mātsaryameva vā/ saṃrambhi bhinnadṛgbhāvaṃ mayi kuryātsa tāmasaḥ//

27. III.29.10 : karmanirhāramuddiśya parasminvā tadarpaṇaṃ/ yajedyaṣṭavyamiti vā pṛthagbhāvaḥ sa sāttvikaḥ//

has not attained devotion beyond the qualities (*nirguṇa*), which contaminate the motive of the devotee. Pure devotion is not vitiated by the personal motives of the devotee, which separate him from Bhagavān and preclude his assimilation to Bhagavān. The qualities vitiate devotion at its most essential point since they introduce a distinction between the devotee and Bhagavān.

In spite of the classification of devotion according to the constituent qualities, there is, however, the *Bhāgavata*'s paradoxical view that hatred can function as a form of saving devotion. The two views are not consistent, at least not apparently, yet the *Bhāgavata* does provide a reconciliation. In canto seven Nārada says that "one should fix one's mind on him through constant enmity, through the absence of enmity, through fear, hatred, or desire."[28] Surely fear and hatred stem from the qualities of inertia (*tamas*) or of action (*rajas*). However, the *Bhāgavata* suggests a solution to this dilemma by means of its teaching on reincarnation and merit. Those who were saved by hatred or fear had in some previous life merited liberation, but because of a flaw, demerit, or curse were condemned to death and rebirth. A special grace was then given to them on account of their merit. The grace was the opportunity to meet Bhagavān Kṛṣṇa or one of his manifestations in combat. As Nārada tells Yudhiṣṭhira: "To free them from the curse, he slew them in that birth, in the form of the hero Rāma...Their sins were destroyed by Kṛṣṇa's discus and they have been freed from the curse."[29]

Characteristics of Devotion

The *Bhāgavata* in no less than twenty passages enumerates the forms and kinds of actions which characterize devotion. It is clear that, while the lists consist of actions, devotion consists of a pure interior attitude of attentive service to Bhagavān. For example in canto three Kapila talks of the following

28. VII.1.25 : tasmādvairānubandhena nirvaireṇa bhayena vā/ snehātkāmena vā yuñjyātkathaṃcinnekṣate pṛthak//

29. VIII.1.44a, 45b : tatrāpi rādhavo bhūtvā nyahanacchāpamuktaye/ rāmavīryaṃ... adhunā śāpanirmuktau kṛṣṇacakrahatāṃhasau//

characteristics of devotion.[30] Devotion completely purifies the mind of the man who does his religious duty faithfully and always performs the prescribed sacrifices without shedding blood. The devotee sees, touches, and worships Bhagavān's image. He sees Bhagavān in all things. Truthful and dispassionate, he is respectful toward great souls and compassionate toward the poor. He is friendly and practices the injunctions of Yoga. He listens to spiritual matters, chants Bhagavān's name, and associates with holy men. Thus he gives up egoism. These moral virtues and spiritual practices are the religious duties (*dharma*) of the *Bhāgavata.* They incorporate the virtues of the holy men of India from the traditions of Yoga, Vedānta, Tantrism, etc. The goal of the religion (*dharma*) of the *Bhāgavata* is stated by Bhagavān in canto eleven: "He visualizes me only, manifested in all beings, both internally and externally, like the sky. With a pure heart, he should see me within himself alone."[31] Positively the *Bhāgavata dharma* brings Bhagavān to the mind unhindered, negatively it eliminates the subtle body, dissolves the realm of primal nature (*prakṛti*), and disperses the effects of the creative energy. This religious practice frees the devotee for devotional service to Bhagavān: "It is my considered opinion that of all the paths to God, to perceive my presence in all beings in one's thought, word, and deed is the most efficacious one."[32]

Among religious practices two are singled out by the *Bhāgavata*'s redactor for special attention: the discipline of action (*karmayoga*) and the ninefold practices of devotion (*navadha bhakti*). Both of these lead to true devotion. The discipline of action is the dedication of the fruits or good results of all actions to God. In canto three Kapila praises the discipline of action in this way. The living are superior to the non-living,

30. Cf. III.29.15-19. In addition characteristics are listed in the following texts : XI.3.23-31; VII.11.8-12; V.5.10-13; III.28.2-7; XI.11.34-41; IV.22.22-25; III.27.6-11; XI.19.20-24; XI.29.9-15; VII.7.30-35; IX.4.18-22; II.3.17-24; VII.5.23-24; III.27.21-23; X.10.38; X.86.46; I.2.14; II.1.5; XII.3.52.

31. XI.29.12 : māmeva sarvabhūteṣu bahirantarapāvṛtam/ īkṣetātmani cātmānaṃ yathā khamamalāśayaḥ//

32. XI.29.19 : ayaṃ hi sarvakalpānāṃ sadhrīcīno mato mama/ madbhāvaḥ sarvabhūteṣu manovākkāya vṛttibhiḥ//

animals are superior to plants, intelligent beings are superior to animals. Superior to all is all the human. Among humans there is a hierarchy: those of caste are superior to those without caste, Brahmans are superior to the other castes, and among the Brahmans the knowers of the *Vedas* are the best. "One who clears up doubts (about the *Vedas*) is better than he who knows the meaning of the *Vedas*; better is he who does his religious duty (*dharma*); better than him is the person who is free from attachment, and does not do his duty for his own gain."[33] Higher still is the one who offers all his actions and their good results to the Lord without any hesitation. "I see no higher being than the person who has dedicated his self and his actions to me; he is without any sense of being an agent and sees all things equally."[34] Such a person treats all things equally because Bhagavān has entered them all with a portion (*kala*) of his being and is their inner Lord. The efficacy of actions lies in the purity of their dedication to Bhagavān. Because the person is present within them as their inner controller, a person's actions are actually Bhagavān's. By means of such an attitude there is a shift of attention from the outer world to the inner self where Bhagavān resides in an intense manner. Such a person is on the threshold of achieving devotion. As Bhagavān Kṛṣṇa says in canto eleven: "While existing in this body, a person strictly follows his own religious duty, purged of impurities, he automatically attains true knowledge or devotion to me engendered in him."[35] When this stage is reached the necessity for the discipline of action disappears, since what was really important, and close to the essence of devotion, was the dedication to Bhagavān.

The Ninefold Practice of Devotion

The *Bhāgavata* places a special emphasis on the ninefold practice of devotion: "The discipline of devotion, by means of

33. III.29.32 : arthajñātsaṃśayacchettā tataḥ śreyānsvakarmakṛt/ muktasaṅgastato bhūyānadogdhā dharmamātmanaḥ

34. III.29.33b, c : mayyarpitātmanaḥ puṃso mayi saṃnyastakarmaṇaḥ/ na paśyāmi paraṃ bhūtamakartuḥ samadarśanāt//

35. XI.20.11 : asmiṃlloke vartamānaḥ svadharmastho'nadhaḥ śuciḥ/ jñānaṃ viśuddhamāpnoti madbhaktiṃ vā yadṛcchayā//

the uttering of Bhagavān's name, etc., is remembered as the highest religious duty (*dharma*) of people in this world."[36] The supreme religion is brought about by the ninefold practice of devotion. The practices are enumerated by Prahlāda in canto seven: (1) hearing, (2) chanting, (3) remembering, (4) service at Bhagavān's feet, (5) offering worship, (6) praising, (7) humility or servitude, (8) friendship, and (9) offering one's self to him.[37]

There are three sets of three here. The first three are traditional Vaiṣṇava practices and are derived from the *Vedas*. The second three are Tantric practices which center around the worship of images. The final three are as much achievements as means. The interaction between the devotee and Bhagavān initiated in the first two sets of practices culminates in unity with him in the last set of three practices. Again the *Bhāgavata* has drawn on various traditions to create a synthetic vision in which the devotee progressively deepens his attachment to Bhagavān until he reaches total surrender.

The path to Bhagavān begins with listening (*śravaṇa*) to his glories. As Śuka says in canto two: "Who, having the bliss of hearing the stories of Hari, would not take delight in them?"[38] Further listening to Bhagavān's glories eradicates the core and cause of all a man's sins: "O Praiseworthy Lord, the purification of the minds of persons with evil propensities does not effectively take place through worship, learning, Vedic studies, acts of charity, penance, or ritual acts as in the minds of persons with pure (*sāttvika*) nature, through the ever-increasing faith and devotion developed by listening to your glory."[39]

The *Bhāgavata* gives chanting (*kīrtana*) a special efficacy for those living in the Kali age.[40] The *Purāṇa* has many instances of

36. VI.3.22 : etāvāneva loke'sminpuṃsāṃ dharmaḥ paraḥ smṛtaḥ/ bhaktiyogo bhagavati tannāmagrahaṇādibhiḥ//

37. VII.5.23: śravaṇaṃ kīrtanaṃ viṣṇoḥ smaraṇaṃ pādasevanam/ arcanaṃ vandanaṃ dāsyaṃ sakhyamātmanivedanam//

38. II.3.12b :...ko nirvṛto harikathāsu ratiṃ na kuryāt//

39. XI.6.9 : śuddhirnṛṇāṃ na tu tathedya durāśayānāṃ vidyaśrutādhyayanadānatapaḥkriyābhiḥ/ sattvātmanāmṛṣabha te yaśasi pravṛddhasacchraddhayā śravaṇasaṃbhṛtayā yathā syāt//

40. Cf. XII.3.52.

devotees singing Bhagavān's glories. In canto seven Prahlāda was so swept up in Bhagavān that "sometimes he would sing loudly."[41] In canto two Śuka elevates singing to one of the highest means of devotion: "O King, this chanting of the name of Hari has been prescribed as the sure means of attaining liberation for those deserving emancipation, and wishing freedom from fear, and for yogins."[42]

Listening and chanting lead to remembering (*smaraṇa*) which reaches the deeper recesses of the being of the devotee. The mind seeks to make conscious for itself that metaphysical presence of Bhagavān, which results from its original emanation from him. The transitory character of material objects becomes apparent and devotion is achieved. "Non-forgetfulness of the lotus feet of Kṛṣṇa annihilates mischief and increases tranquility, purity of mind, devotion to the Highest Self, and knowledge coupled with wisdom and dispassion."[43]

The Tantric practices of the second set of three practices of devotion reflect the reality of the manifestations of Bhagavān within the realm of primal nature (*prakṛti*). Bhagavān is present in the image in a special manner and thus the material thing is worthy of worship: "One who is yoked by means of devotion with sincerity should worship me as his preceptor with the materials (*dravya*) of worship, in an image, prepared ground, the fire, the sun, water, the heart, or in a twice-born person."[44]

The final three practices are built on the first six. Servitude or humility (*dāsya*) is an interior attitude central to devotion.[45] Friendship (*sakhya*) results when Bhagavān, sure of the devotee's humility, allows him to feel the grace of God. God is not just his master but an intimate friend with whom the devotee feels familiar. Offering one's self to Bhagavān or total surrender

41. VII.4.39b :... udgāyati kvacit//

42. II.1.11 : etannirvidyamānānāmicchatāmakutobhayam/ yogināṃ nṛpa nirṇītaṃ harernāmānukīrtanam//

43. XII.12.54 : avismṛtiḥ kṛṣṇapadāravindayoḥ kṣiṇotyabhadrāṇi śamaṃ tanoti ca/ sattvasya śuddhiṃ paramātmabhaktiṃ jñānaṃ ca vijñānavirāga-yuktam//

44. XI.27.9 : arcāyāṃ sthaṇḍile'gnau vā sūrye vāpsu hṛdi dvije/dravyeṇa bhaktiyukto'rcetsvaguruṃ māmamāyayā//

45. Cf. VII.9.50.

(*ātmanivedana*), which is the culmination of devotion, brings the devotee to union with Bhagavān: "When having renounced all activities a mortal dedicates himself (niveditātmā) to me, he is chosen by me; attaining immortality, he is qualified to become one with me, sharing my divine powers."[46]

Two additional practices which are forms of devotion and which overlap with and are associated with the ninefold practice of devotion may be treated here. The first is the repetition of the divine name (*nāmajapa*). The place of God's name occupies an important place in the ninefold practice of devotion, but the *Bhāgavata* also refers to *nāmajapa* in many other places. The name of God has an intrinsic glory and numinous power. In the story of Ajāmila even the mere sound of God's name is salvific. Ajāmila is delivered from his sins by a single utterance of the sound 'Nārāyaṇa', even though accidental. He intended, while lying on his death bed, to call his son who had that name to his side: "Just as medicine which is most powerful when consumed produces its effect, so muttering the name casually even when one is unaware produces its effect for the Self."[47]

The name of God has such power that it awakens the ever-present Bhagavān. Its repetition in the Kali age is effective in bringing peace in the midst of sin and vice. There is no greater gain for those lost in the world of misery than the chanting of the divine names "from which one finds the highest tranquility and the cycle of death and rebirth (*saṃsāra*) disappears."[48]

The second practice is the worship of the preceptor (*guru*). For instance, Prabuddha tells King Nimi in the eleventh canto that someone who wants to know the highest good should resort to a preceptor who is versed in the *Vedas* and has realized the Highest Brahman and thus is free from attachment. "Under the guru whom one should regard as one's own self one should learn the religious duty of a devotee, by service to the guru; so that Hari who is the self of the universe and confers self-realization,

46. XI.29.34 : martyo yadā tyaktasamastakarmā niveditātmā vicikīrṣito me/ tadā'mṛtatvaṃ pratipadyamāno mayātmabhūyāya ca kalpate vai//

47. VI.2.19 : yathā'gadaṃ vīryatamamupayuktaṃ yadṛcchayā/ ajānato'-pyātmaguṇaṃ kuryānmantro'pyudāhṛtaḥ//

48. XI.5.37 : nahyataḥ paramo lābho dehināṃ bhrāmyatāmiha / yato vindeta paramāṃ śāntiṃ naśyati saṃsṛtiḥ//

becomes pleased with him."[49] In this way the preceptor is the representative of the divine preceptor, Bhagavān Kṛṣṇa. Kṛṣṇa also himself acts as a preceptor in the eleventh canto when he teaches Uddhava the ways of devotion. In the tenth canto he gives a high place to the preceptor when he tells Sudāma that he, "the Self of all beings is not as pleased with sacrifices nor the investiture with the sacred, thread, penance, silence. etc. as he is with service to a preceptor...It is by the grace of the preceptor especially that a man is given peace and attains perfection."[50] If it is thus with a human preceptor, how much more when one's preceptor is Bhagavān Kṛṣṇa himself.

The ninefold practices of devotion with their associated customs are centered at each stage on a personal God, who is progressively transformed from an impersonal Brahman into the Supreme Person, Bhagavān. The Divine is always within the devotee awaiting an awakening. The ninefold devotion is a prerequisite as a means, though subject to the grace of Bhagavān, to the bestowal of the end of devotion which is Bhagavān himself.

Yoga and Knowledge

The *Bhagavad Gītā* uses the term *yoga* to denote a spiritual path or discipline.[51] It uses the prefixes *karma*, *jñāna*, and *bhakti* to indicate different paths. However, Patañjali systematized *yoga* as a specific technique in its own right which severs the individual spirit (*puruṣa*) from any connection with the twenty-four categories (*tattva*). The *Bhāgavata* draws on both tradition, mixes them, and at times keeps them separate from its treatment of devotion. As an inclusive *Purāṇa*, the *Bhāgavata* neglects, though at some cost to consistency, no part of Vaiṣṇava wisdom. Devotion is at times practically assimilated to the way of knowledge (*jñāna*) and/or to Yoga, but in the end the

49. XI.3.22 : tatra bhāgavatāndharmān śikṣedgurvātmadaivataḥ amāyayānuvṛttyā yaistuṣyedātmātmado hariḥ//

50. X.80.34,43b : nāhamijyāprajātibhyāṃ tapasopaśamena vā/ tuṣyeyaṃ sarvabhūtātmā guruśuśrūṣayā yathā//...guroranugraheṇaiva pumānpūrṇaḥ praśāntaye//

51. Cf. *Bhagavad Gītā* III.3.

Bhāgavata distinguishes devotion from them and establishes the superiority of devotion over the other disciplines of salvation (*sādhana*).

In many passages the *Bhāgavata* postulates the need to control the senses as a propaedeutic to devotion to Bhagavān. In canto three Kapila speaks of the entrapment of the individual spirit (*puruṣa*) within the qualities of primal nature (*prakṛti*), which results in egoism and attachment to action and the world of the creative energy. The egoism and attachment are not real but illusory. Thus he prescribes devotion as a means to free the devotee from these evils. "Therefore gradually through the discipline of devotion (*bhaktiyoga*) and through intense non-attachment (*virakti*) one should bring under control the mind which is attached to the path of sensual enjoyment."[52] Thus through devotion a man becomes a yogin and performs all the practices of Yoga. He becomes even-minded and unattached and realizes the Self. One who is controlled by his senses and their gratification cannot follow the path of devotion until they are brought under control. The path of yoga, which is here just barely distinguished from the yoga of devotion, is reminiscent of Patañjali's eightfold Yoga. The highest goal of this exercise is the realization of non-dual Brahman.[53] The devotee finds that his true self is the Self and that the eightfold Yoga removes the obstacles to that realization.

This *yoga* is called by Śrīdhara *vaiṣṇavayoga*, and is treated in detail in chapters twenty-eight and twenty-nine of canto three where Kapila teaches his mother about "the character of Yoga, which has some object to subsist on (*sabīja*), by practicing which the mind becomes tranquil and pure and attains the path of truth."[54] In order to dissolve the twenty-four categories, one applies external restraint (*yama*) and internal control (*niyama*).[55] This kind of *yoga* is *sabīja*, that is, its goal is a deep

52. III.27.5 : ata eva śanaiścittaṃ prasaktamasatāṃ pathi/ bhaktiyogena tīvreṇa viraktyā ca nayedvaśam//

53. Cf. III.27.11.

54. III.28.1 : yogasya lakṣaṇaṃ vakṣye sabījasya nṛpātmaje/ mano yenaiva vidhinā prasannaṃ yāti satpatham//

55. Cf. III.28.2-5a and XI.19.33-34.

meditation (*samādhi*) with an object. Its meditation leaves behind the unreal sense world and centers on the real object, Bhagavān. A deep meditation without an object (*nirbīja*), contentless concentration, however, is the goal of Vaiṣṇava Yoga: "Just as a flame is extinguished, the mind immediately obtains extinction (*nirvāṇa*), when it is indifferent, detached from sense objects, and freed from its support; the spirit (*puruṣa*) then experiences the Self as one, without the distinctions of subject and object and free from the flow of the qualities."[56] The person is free from sorrow and distress. He, "having established himself in this glory, which is beyond pleasure and pain, by means of this last restraint of the mind, realizes the essential nature of the Self and transfers the agency of the pleasure and pain from himself to ahaṃkāra, which is not ultimately real."[57] Thus there is a complete surrender of the true interior self, stripped of its mental accretions, to Brahman and a realization of their unity. In this way the practice of Yoga is put to a Vedāntic purpose.

In chapter twenty-nine of the third canto, the *Bhāgavata* states that "the *yoga* of devotion and Yoga have been described by me; by either of these two the individual spirit (*puruṣa*) can attain the Person (*puruṣa*)."[58] Subsequently there is a similar affirmation in chapter thirty-two : "The *yoga* of knowledge and the *yoga* characterized devotion which is without qualities directed to me both have the same goal, which is signified by the word 'Bhagavān.'"[59] Thus Yoga and the *yoga* of devotion, and the *yoga* of knowledge and devotion, lead to the same goal, though each path influences how that goal is perceived, whether

56. III.28.35 : muktāśrayaṃ yarhi nirviṣayaṃ viraktaṃ nirvāṇamṛcchati manaḥ sahasā yathā'rciḥ/ātmānamatra puruṣo vyavadhānamekamanvīkṣate pratinivṛttaguṇapravāhaḥ//

57. III.28.36 : so'pyetayā caramayā manaso nivṛttyā tasminmahimnyavasitaḥ sukhaduḥkhabāhye/ hetutvamapyasati kartari duḥkhayoryatsvātmanvidhatta upalabdhaparātmakāṣṭhaḥ//

58. III.29.35 : bhaktiyogaśca yogaśca mayā mānavyudīritaḥ/ yayorekatareṇaiva puruṣaḥ puruṣaṃ vrajet//

59. III.32.32 : jñānayogaśca manniṣṭho nairguṇyo bhaktilakṣaṇaḥ/ dvayorapyeka evārtho bhagavacchabdalakṣaṇaḥ//

as Brahman, the Highest Self, or Bhagavān. The latter text suggests that Bhagavān is the primary identity of this goal, though subject to a more impersonal perception or realization in Yoga and the path of knowledge. Also it seems that even devotion, when considered in close conjunction with these paths, assimilates their characteristics so that Bhagavān becomes tinged with the impersonal overtones of Brahman. As S. Bhaṭṭācārya remarks: "The *jñāna yoga* of the *Bhāgavata* forges a remarkable compromise between Patañjali and the Upaniṣads..."[60]

In canto eleven the *Bhāgavata* associates each of the three *yogas* of the *Bhagavad Gītā* with a different type of person. The discipline of knowledge is suitable for those who find no use in ritual action, while the discipline of action is effective for those who still find the ritual actions helpful. But "the yoga of devotion is conducive to liberation for the person in whom by good fortune has sprouted a faith in my stories, etc. and who is neither disgusted with nor deeply attached to the performance of acts."[61] Here devotion is more clearly distinguished from the paths of knowledge and of action, and by extension from the eightfold Yoga, than in the previous passages. Devotion steers a middle course between indulgence in and attachment to the realm of the senses. In this way the *Bhāgavata* gives a positive value to this world so that "heavenly beings and demons desire to be born in this world, which leads to liberation by both knowledge and devotion, which is not possible in their world."[62] The devotee neither flees the world nor seeks its rewards. The implication is that he will need to use his senses, properly of course, in the various practices of devotion.

When the *Bhāgavata* presents the discipline of devotion as a mosaic of devotion, detachment and knowledge, it would seem to be carefully delimiting the scope of the discipline of devotion.

60. Bhaṭṭācārya, *The Philosophy of the Śrīmad-Bhāgavata*, II, 106.

61. XI.20.8 : yadṛcchayā satkathādau jātaśraddhastu yaḥ pumān/ na nirviṇṇo nāstisakto bhaktiyogo'sya siddhidaḥ//

62. XI.20.12: svargino'pyetamicchanti lokaṃ nirayiṇastathā/ sādhakaṃ jñānabhaktibhyāmubhayaṃ tadasādhakam//

It is as if it feared to envisage devotion as a feeling (*anubhāva*) or as love (*preman*). If devotion is attachment to Bhagavān, the detachment from all that distracts from that attachment is necessary. One must also know the object of attachment. Thus the organic association of devotion with datachment and knowledge is proposed for the discipline of devotion (*bhaktiyoga*). As Kapila says in canto three: "The person with his self joined to knowledge, non-attachment and devotion, realizes his self to be absolute, distinct from and beyond primal nature, immutable, self-luminous, atomic, indivisible, passive, and finds primal nature powerless."[63] Knowledge and detachment, in fact, need devotion to get beyond the sphere of primal nature (*prakṛti*). Canto twelve in a passage near the end of the *Purāṇa* says that "in this *Purāṇa* has been considered withdrawal from and cessation of all actions accompanied by knowledge, renunciation, and devotion; the one who listens to it, reads it constantly, and considers it with devotion is liberated."[64] These three disciplines or paths allow the *Bhāgavata* to close the gap between the devotee and the object of his devotion.

However, the *Bhāgavata* is not content to limit devotion to the elitist confines of asceticism with its complicated and difficult Yoga nor to the Brahmanic exclusiveness of the path of knowledge. Devotion is sufficient. Kṛṣṇa tells Uddhava in canto eleven that the yogin who is yoked to him by means of devotion has no need of knowledge nor detachment. All that is gained from knowledge, detachment, and Yoga "the person who is devoted to me quickly attains by means of the discipline of devotion to me whether it be heaven, beatitude, or my abode."[65] This way of devotion is special because it has been revealed by Kṛṣṇa.[66] Just as devotion puts a new light on action since it is the interior attitude that counts, so knowledge is given a new significance. As S. Bhaṭṭācārya comments: "If the goal of the Upaniṣadic knowledge is the dissolution of the

63. III.25.17-18 : tadā puruṣa ātmānaṃ kevalaṃ prakṛteḥ param/ nirantaraṃ svayaṃjyotiraṇimānamakhaṇḍitam// jñānavairāgyayuktena bhaktiyuktena cātmanā/ paripaśyatyudāsīnaṃ prakṛtiṃ ca hataujasam//

64. XII.13.18b : tatra jñānavirāgabhaktisahitaṃ naiṣkarmyamāviṣkṛtaṃ tacchṛṇvanvipaṭhanvicāraṇaparo bhaktyā vimucyennaraḥ//

65. XI.20.33 : sarvaṃ madbhaktiyogena madbhakto labhate'ñjasā/ svargāpavargaṃ maddhāma kathaṃcidyadi vāñchati//

66. Cf. XI.20.37.

individual to Brahman, the infinite, then the rigour of knowledge seems to dry up the sap of life. Self-extinction can hardly be a cherishable goal."[67] The *Bhāgavata* has edged close to the abyss of a non-dualism with no qualities (*nirviśeṣādvaita*) and then backed away, recoiling from the 'Pelagian' self-centeredness of Yoga and the aridity of the path of knowledge. Instead of self-effort, the *Bhāgavata* in other passages offers a path of grace.

Superiority of Devotion

Devotion is a simple path to Bhagavān and he makes it easier. Maitreya in canto three says: "What is difficult to be achieved when the Lord of all blessings is pleased ? Enough with things of insignificant value. The Supreme Lord, the Dweller in the hearts of all, of his own accord, confers the highest state on those who are devoted to him without any ulterior motive."[68] The Lord is present within the devotee and knows his inner attitude. He radiates his affection for men. But by oneself it is difficult to overcome the deluding power of Bhagavān's creative energy (*māyā*). "Only those can go beyond and understand the real nature of God's creative energy, which is very difficult to cross, if the infinite Lord is gracious to them, and these devotees, with all their heart and self, sincerely resort to his feet. Such persons are free from the idea of 'I and mine', which are the food of dogs and jackals."[69] Only the one who has been blessed by Kṛṣṇa's grace (*prasāda*) can realize the greatness of Bhagavān.[70] The Lord chooses his devotees. These he allows to see himself as he is, that is, as one with his devotees.

By means of his creative energy (*māyā*) Bhagavān creates, maintains, and dissolves the universe and the humans within it. This normal cycle is caused and abetted by the decline of virtue

67. Bhaṭṭācarya, *The Philosophy of the Śrīmad-Bhāgavata*, II, 111.

68. III.13.49 : tasminprasanne sakalāśisāṃ prabhau kiṃ durlabhaṃ tābhiralaṃ lavātmabhiḥ/ananyadṛṣṭyā bhajatāṃ guhāśayaḥ svayaṃ vidhatte svagatiṃ paraḥ parām//

69. II.7.42: yeṣāṃ sa eva bhagavāndayayedanantaḥ sarvātmanāśritapado yadi nirvyalīkam/ te dustarāmatitaranti ca devamāyāṃ naiṣāṃ mamāhamiti dhīḥ śvaśṛgālabhakṣye//

70. Cf. X.14.29-30.

and the growth of sin, which are the conditions for Hari's special appearances as *avatāras*. Man's sin is a *felix culpa* because it induces Bhagavān to present himself before men as the perfect object of devotion, Kṛṣṇa. Man is ignorant and sins, Kṛṣṇa saves. "For the activity of his creative energy brings about the continuance, origin, and destruction of a person while his grace is intended to bring self-realization through the cessation (of the creative energy)."[71] By the grace of Kṛṣṇa the cycle of death and rebirth (*saṃsāra*) is broken, birth does not reoccur and the Self is realized.

Because it comes directly from an impulse of Bhagavān, devotion surpasses and replaces every other discipline of salvation (*sādhana*). Worship heals the aberrations of the flesh better than other methods. As Nārada says in canto one: "The self which is continuously afflicted by desire and greed is not calmed by the paths of Yoga, with abstentions, etc. as directly as through service to Mukunda."[72] The other disciplines accomplish natural goals. Bhagavān is reached by centering one's heart on him. Because there is no higher goal, there is no more exalted means. Means and goal coalesce.

Speculative knowledge on impersonal Brahman and action with a motive are useful only if suffused with the spirit of devotion. The *Bhāgavata* thus takes two approaches to the other disciplines of salvation. The first employs them in the service of the devotee striving to reach Bhagavān. In this case devotion is seen as the goal, which may be reached by any method as long as it is reached. In the second approach the *Bhāgavata* stresses the efficacy of devotion as a method. The goal is such that a simple method of attention to Bhagavān is all that is necessary. By either approach Bhagavān is reached, though the simplicity of the latter approach makes it more available in the Kali age.

In fact in one passage in canto eleven, the *Bhāgavata* speaks of devotion both as a goal and as a means, both as cause and as

71. IX.24.58: yanmāyāceṣṭhitaṃ puṃsaḥ sthityutpattyapyāya hi/ anugrahastannivṛtterātmalābhāya ceṣyate//

72. I.6.36: yamādibhiryogapathaiḥ kāmalobhahato muhuḥ/ mukundasevayā yadvattathātmā'ddhā na śāmyati//

effect. Devotion is a discipline which leads to a permanent state, devotion. Prabuddha says to King Nimi that "remembering and reminding each other of Hari who destroys falsehood in a moment, their devotion (means) turns into devotion (goal), the hair of their bodies stands up from joy."[73] Devotion helps the devotee cross over the creative energy of Bhagavān and leave behind an existence contaminated by the three qualities for a way of existence which transcends the production of the individual without at the same time negating his individuality.

Liberation

We have seen in Chapter I that liberation (*mukti*) is one of the characteristics or topics of a *Purāṇā*.[74] It is defined in canto two as "the abandoning of the unreal form, and staying in his essential nature."[75] The individual self's connection with a body is an assumed form which acts in and is bound to the world. At liberation this is left behind. The proper form is the realization of oneness with Bhagavān. A similar description of liberation is given in canto three: "When he sees himself freed from the influence of the elements, senses, the qualities, and the mind, when he abides in me by my own form, then he enjoys self-mastery.[76] Here liberation is considered as the dissolution of the Sāṃkhya categories back to their original latent state.

Thus it seems that the *Bhāgavata* has several versions of what the final goal of human beings is. One version describes the apparently impersonal absorption into the Absolute. Another version describes service at the lotus feet of Bhagavān, or loving devotion, as the goal. In the first case, however, it must be remembered that the individual self eternally exists or subsists with Brahman in an elusive subtle state, even in the most radical state of dissolution. At the same time, even in the second description, it is not a heaven, which is described here as the goal of devotion, but a state of being.

73. XI.3.31 : smarantaḥ smārayantaśca mitho'ghaughaharaṃ harim/ bhaktyā samjātayā bhaktyā bibhratyutpulakāṃ tanum//

74. Cf. II.10.1 and XII.7.9-10.

75. II.10.6b : muktirhitvānyathārūpaṃ svarūpeṇa vyavasthitiḥ//

76. III.9.33 : yadā rahitamātmānaṃ bhūtendriyaguṇāśayaiḥ/ svarūpeṇa mayopetaṃ paśyansvārājyamṛcchati//

The *Bhāgavata,* indeed, is much clearer about what is not the goal or salvation of human beings than what is. It rejects five traditional kinds of beatitude as undesirable. In canto three Kapila says that these kinds of beatitude do not attract the devotee once he has set his eyes on the goal of devotion, which is beyond the qualities of primal nature.[77] The state which is finally attained is beyond the qualities; the five states which are rejected are within the sphere of the qualities. They do not take the seeker beyond the qualities. They are incomplete dissolutions of the phenomenal self with its physical appurtenances. The five rejected states are : (1) residence in the Vaikuṇṭha heaven with Bhagavān (*sālokya*), (2) the possession of divine powers (*sārṣṭi*), (3) living in Bhagavān's presence (*sāmīpya*), (4) the possession of the divine form (*sārūpya*), and (5) absorption into his being (*ekātva*). The latter in this context must mean an absorption compatible with remaining within the sphere of the qualities. None of these states of beatitude can compare with the simple state of devotion, which is a state of union (left finally unexplained, though beyond the qualities) with Bhagavān : "That only is called the final discipline of devotion by which one overcomes the three qualities and attains my state."[78] In canto nine each of these types of beatitude is contained within devotion: "Fully satisfied by service to me, they do not desire the four types (of beatitude), such as residence, etc. which are attained by service to me. How could they desire these other things which are ravaged by time?"[79] Here the states of beatitude are attained unwittingly by the devotee. They are supererogatory. Instead of being explained as subject to the qualities, they are described as subject to time. The states always involve, even in their highest degree, some form of death and rebirth. To the extent that they are not final these states of beatitude are actually states of bondage.

77. Cf. III.29.13-14.

78. III.29.14 : sa eva bhaktiyogākhya ātyantika udāhṛtaḥ/ yenātivrajya triguṇaṃ madbhāvāyopapadyate//

79. IX.4.67 : matsevayā pratītaṃ ca sālokyādicatuṣṭayam/ necchanti sevayā pūrṇāḥ kuto'nyatkālavidrutam//. Only four states are mentioned here probably sārṣṭi is omitted.

The states of beatitude do however have a medicinal function. Kṛṣṇa says in the eleventh canto that the promise of reward in these states is "introductory to beatitude just as a remedy (for the stomach) lead to an appetite."[80] Each type of beatitude is thus a new phase of emancipation, which must be deepened, lest it become a bondage and lead to death and rebirth.

Without describing this final state of devotion except to say that it is blissful, the *Bhāgavata* says that it takes the devotee out of the cycle of death and rebirth (*saṃsāra*). Death and rebirth are then extinguished. The devotee "never returns in any way to the cycle of death and rebirth like the others; he remembers the embracing of Mukunda's feet, and attracted to that pleasure, he does not want to lose it."[81] Mukunda, the epithet of Bhagavān, means bestower of liberation. Once Bhagavān has made himself known, the devotee will never abandon him; having reached the final goal, which is union with Bhagavān himself, there is no way metaphsically to return to *saṃsāra*.[82]

However, the *Bhāgavata*, in some passages, separates itself even from this doctrine of the liberation through devotion from the cycle of death and rebirth.[83] The devotee might be tempted to seek this liberation and therefore vitiate the purity of his devotion to Bhagavān. Devotion must always be disinterested. As Kṛṣṇa says in canto eleven: "He who has been devoted to me no more desires the position of the highest, the realm of the great Indra, power over the universe, rulership of the underworlds, yogic powers, the state of not being reborn, nothing apart from me."[84] Free from expectation, the devotee will get everything from Bhagavān. Bhagavān is even under an obligation of sorts to the devotee since the devotee provides Bhagavān

80. XI.21.23b : śreyovivakṣayā proktaṃ yathā bhaiṣajyarocanam//

81. 1.5.19: na vai jano jātu kathaṃcanāvrajenmukundasevyanyavadaṅga saṃsṛtim/ smaranmukundāṃghryupaguhanaṃ punarvihātumicchenna rasagraho yataḥ//

82. Cf. III.25.39-41, 43-44.

83. Cf. VI.3.22 and VII.7.55.

84. XI.14.14 : na pārameṣṭhyaṃ na mahendradhiṣṇyaṃ na sārvabhaumaṃ na rasādhipatyam/ na yogasidhīrapunarbhavaṃ vā mayyarpitātmecchati madvinānyat//

with the opportunity to bestow a participation in his perfect bliss.

What unites all these passages, regardless of terminological nuance and diversity, is the *Bhāgavata*'s unrelenting non-dualism. Devotion and/or the disciplines of knowledge, Yoga, and detachment, or devotion alone, are grounded in the inclusive unity of Bhagavān. While championing the path of devotion, the *Bhāgavata* makes a place for Yoga and the paths of knowledge and datachment, since they lead to Bhagavān.[85] It has gone over backward in accommodating the vision of a Brahman without qualities which arises from the path of knowledge and from some forms of devotion. Yet the *Bhāgavata* qualifies this stark vision. Through all these paths, the seekers "attain Bhagavān by these both as 'without qualities' and 'with qualities.' "[86] Both descriptions are non-dualist, but the *Bhāgavata* favors the latter because on account of its commitment to devotion it cannot renounce the non-dual Bhagavān's evolution of the qualities, etc. from himself.

Bondage comes from duality, which is always the illusion of separateness from Bhagavān. Mastery of the individual self's illusions through devotion overcomes this sense of duality, which can only be a 'sense' of duality: "Until by means of self-realization one determines that this is illusion, there will continue that duality which follows from the mistake about this."[87] Perhaps some without postulating a metaphysical unity may consider liberation as a moral attainment of unity. But this is not the way of the *Bhāgavata* for which the experience of unity with Bhagavān is not possible without the reality of actual unity with him. Because the devotee comes from Bhagavān, never ceases to be from Bhagavān, is always ruled from within by Bhagavān, he can return to Bhagavān from whom he is never really, only illusorily, separated. The separation is real for the devotee but not for Bhagavān. The *Bhāgavata* is willing, as we have seen above, to forego the feeling or the experience of unity with Bhagavān, if that experience itself would hinder the reality of

85. Cf. III.32.32.
86. III.32.36b : iyate bhagavānebhih saguṇo nirguṇaḥ svadṛk//
87. VII.12.10 : kalpayitvātmanā yāvadābhāsamidamīśvaraḥ/ dvaitaṃ tāvanna virametṭato hyasya viparyayaḥ/

unity. Illusion, attachment, and the experience of unity may hinder the reality of unity.

The type of devotion which is built on or accommodated to knowledge, Yoga, and detachment, reenforces the experience of non-duality. This devotion edges toward an experience and postulation of Brahman without qualities. It is tempted to forego the personal Bhagavān with qualities. Yet the *Bhāgavata*'s redactor was a member of a group of forward looking Brahmans who were experiencing the fire and ardor of a new form of devotion. In its discursive passages the *Bhāgavata* is conservative; the devotion it teaches looks back to the *Bhagavad Gītā* and to Yoga. Yet in its rich narratives, the redactor reveals a new vision of an emotional devotion which raises Bhagavān Kṛṣṇa's dalliance with the cowherd girls of Vṛndāvana as a paradigm. This ecstatic devotion will be treated in the next chapter.

CHAPTER VI

DEVOTION: THE REALITY OF THE DEVOTEE

The Āḷvārs

Along with the type of devotion associated with knowledge and detachment, which is derived from the *Bhagavad Gītā,* there is in the *Bhāgavata* the emotional and ecstatic devotion which at the time it was written was chiefly associated with the Vaiṣṇavas of South India.[1] This type of devotion makes a conscious use of erotic love-symbolism, which had little place in the religious tradition based on the *Vedas* and the *Upaniṣads.* Devotion as mystical love between the devotee and God arose in the Tamil country about the sixth century among both Śaiva and Vaiṣṇava devotees. Against elitist Buddhism and Jainism, which had been prominent in South India, and probably also against the Brahmanic ritualism filtering in from the north, South India developed an intense devotion to Śiva and to Viṣṇu in his Kṛṣṇa form. This devotion had a mass appeal for those of low caste and for those who could not, or would not, sever their relations with the ordinary world, and thus devotion filled a religious vacuum. As G. Yocum asserts:

> But while the political situation may have played a part in the rise of *bhakti,* basically the Tamil *bhakti* movement, in view of the other religions' irrelevence to the life of the common man, was an attempt to find a form of religious expression and practice within the context of both indigenous

1. See Friedhelm Hardy, *Viraha Bhakti : The Early History of Kṛṣṇa Devotion in South India* (Delhi : Oxford University, 1983).

ideas and pan-Indian traditions which would be meaningful to a wide range of people at a fairly deep level.[2]

The Tamil Vaiṣṇava saints, the Āḷvārs, made a special use of the language of the love and sexual feeling between a man and a woman to portray the experience which they had with God. The union, separation, and abandonment of lovers suggest the power and poignancy of the saints' devotion to God. For example, in this poem by Nammāḷvār, one of the greatest of the Āḷvārs, the imagery of the separation of lovers symbolizes his agony in being separated from God:

Evening has come, He has not.
And the kine are wriggling in content,
For the bulls, bells jingling,
Have mated with them.
The cruel flutes are prating.
Within the bright, bright jasmine buds,
And the blue lily
The bee is fluttering and dancing.
The sea breaks open, leaping up to the sky and
cries and cries.
What is it that I can say?
How can I escape and save myself,
Here, without Him?[3]

The devotees go beyond the imagery and allegory of erotic poetry, which had deep roots in Tamil culture. Their devotion, their active experience of Bhagavān, as we shall see in the *Bhāgavata*, was deeply personal and, at times, sexual. These experiences are in conflict with a strong ethical tradition, and they are of such power that the devotees sublimate their experiences by means of allegorical interpretations.

Ch. Vaudeville suggests that there was an early influence on South Indian religion and culture from the Sufis, which "cannot

2. Glenn Yocum, "Shrines, Shamanism, and Love Poetry : Elements in the Emergence of Popular Tamil Bhakti," *Journal of the American Academy of Religion*, XLI (March 1973), 4.

3. *Ibid.*, p. 15.

be ruled out chronologically, whilst geographical and historical circumstances give it some amount of probability."[4] The intense Tamil theism, whether Śaiva or Vaiṣṇava, would at this early date, seventh or eighth century, have been inclined to see Islamic monotheism, especially in its mystical form, as an ally, rather than as a rival. The Sufis stressed the irreversible love-relationship between God and the human soul, and the need for absolute self-surrender and intense longing on the part of the believer. For example, the Sufi Zaid says in one of his sermons: "O Brothers, will you not weep with desire for God? He who weeps with desire for his Lord, how could he be deprived of his vision?"[5]

Among the Vaiṣṇava traditions being brought in from the north of India were those of the *Harivaṃśa* and the *Viṣṇu Purāṇa* concerning the life and loves of Kṛṣṇa Vāsudeva. The Āḷvārs make abundant use of these romantic exploits especially those illustrating the themes of the bliss of union and of the fear of separation, bringing them to the greatest development prior to the *Bhāgavata*. The tension between these two, the proximity to and the distance from Bhagavān, is the root of the Āḷvārs' devotion and led them to prefer the perfection of devotion to the final emancipation of the path of knowledge. Thus in the context of Tamil devotion, a group of ascetical devotees composed or redacted the *Bhāgavata Purāṇa* in Sanskrit, infusing the dynamic elements of emotional and ecstatic devotion into the inherited matrix of the quiet, peaceful devotion stemming from the *Bhagavad Gītā*.

4. Ch. Vaudeville, "Evolution of Love-Symbolism in Bhagavatism," *Journal of the American Oriental Society*, LXXXII (March 1962), 35. That there was a Christian influence on the development of *bhakti* and of the Kṛṣṇa legends has been widely suggested, yet there is no conclusive evidence. Some exaggerated claims (by William Jones, B. Seal, R. G. Bhandarkar, N. Macnicol and others) have been refuted by Hemchandra Raychaudhuri, *Materials for the Study of the Early History of the Vaishnava Sect* (New Delhi : Oriental Books Reprint Corporation, 1975). Of course, Christianity would have had an indirect influence, through Islam, if Vaudeville's suggestion is correct.

5. *Ibid.*, p. 36.

Ecstatic Devotion

The *Bhāgavata* often describes devotion in terms of intoxication and ecstasy. In canto one Nārada tells how his mission began in an intense devotional experience. In an uninhabited forest Nārada sat in the shelter of a Peepul tree and contemplated within his heart all that he had heard about the Self who was supposed to reside within the individual self. As he meditated, "with my mind overpowered with affection and tears flowing from my eyes from longing, Hari gradually appeared in my heart." He was overwhelmed with happiness and "transfixed with love (*preman*) and absorbed in an ocean of bliss."[6] He could see neither himself nor the Lord. Disturbed by the disappearance of Hari, he tried again to concentrate his mind but could not regain the vision. Unsatisfied, he was deeply disturbed. In Nārada's intense emotional experience he was overpowered by love (*preman*). *Preman* expresses "the ardent tenderness and fondness especially between two lovers."[7] Thus Nārada had felt love for Bhagavān, but then felt the pangs of the withdrawal of this beautiful form of his beloved. This desolation of being separated from one's lover purifies, as Hari tells Nārada: "O virtuous one, this form has been revealed only once to arouse desire in you. The devotee gradually gives up all that resides in his heart."[8] Thus here the devotional experience has had the same result as a process of Yoga, the giving up of all that is unnecessary in the heart.

The ecstasy and love described are but one exceptional phase in the life of Nārada who was an ascetic, yogin, and devotee. He is still a representative of the *Bhāgavata*'s conservative strand of devotion. Prahlāda is an unambiguous example of the new type of devotee. In canto seven his story is told. Aside from the cowherd girls in canto ten, Prahlāda is one of the foremost of the devotees, a *mahābhāgavata*.[9] He learned about devotion

6. I.6.17-18a: dhyāyataścaraṇāmbhojaṃ bhāvanirjitacetasā/ autkaṇṭhyāśrukalākṣasya hṛdyāsīnme śanairhariḥ// premātibharanirbhinnapulakāṅgo' tinirvṛtaḥ/

7. Vaudeville, "Evolution of Love-Symbolism in Bhagavatism," p. 39.

8. I.6.23 : sakṛdyaddarśitaṃ rūpametatkāmāya te'nagha/matkāmaḥ śanakaiḥ sādhuḥ sarvānmuñcati hṛcchayān//

9. Cf. VII.7.10a.

while a fetus in his mother's womb, when Nārada was teaching her. She forget the teaching but Prahlāda remembered. As a boy of five he taught devotion to his childhood companions. His devotion is an inward contemplation of Viṣṇu, but it also takes vivid, ecstatic expression outwardly: "Having as a child put aside his playthings, his mind absorbed in Kṛṣṇa, he appeared like a dunce. His self was possessed by Kṛṣṇa, as though by a spirit, he did not know the ordinary world."[10] He was never conscious of the things he was doing, so deep was his attention centered on Kṛṣṇa. "Now he would cry, his mind seized by the thought of Vaikuṇṭha, now he would laugh, delighting in thought of him, now he would sing aloud, now he would shriek with open throat, now dance banishing all bashfulness, blushing, imagining himself to be one with him and merged in him, he would imitate him."[11] Then he would sit quietly, happy and full of the tears of bliss brought by constant love.

In canto eleven a similar devotee is described by Kavi, the sage: "The man who has vowed such conduct develops love for him by singing the names of his beloved, his heart melting in devotion, loudly laughing and weeping, screaming, singing, dancing like one possessed, flaunting the world."[12] So intense is his mad devotion, he bows to all in sight, thinking them to be forms of Bhagavān. "At one time these three appear together, devotion, realization of the Highest Lord, and aversion to other things, in him who has resigned himself to the Lord, just as one who eats is satisfied, is nourished, and gets relief from hunger with each morsel."[13] The devotee thus extends his love and reverence for Hari to all his creatures, who are the body (śarīra)

10. VII.4.37 : nyastakrīḍanako bālo jaḍavattanmanastayā/ kṛṣṇagrahagṛhītātmā na veda jagadīdṛśam/

11. VII.4.39-40 : kvacidrudati vaikuṇṭhacintāśabalacetanaḥ/ kvaciddhasati taccintāhlāda udgāyati kvacit// nadati kvacidutkaṇṭho vilajjo nṛtyati kvacit/ kvacittadbhāvanāyuktastanmayo'nucakāra ha//

12. XI.2.40 : evaṃvrataḥ svapriyanāmakīrtyā jātānurāgo drutacitta uccaiḥ/ hasatyatho roditi rauti gāyatyunmādavannṛtyati lokabāhyaḥ//

13. XI.2.42 : bhaktiḥ pareśānubhavo viraktiranyatra caiṣa trika ekakālaḥ/ prapadyamānasya yathā'śnataḥ syustuṣṭiḥ puṣṭiḥ kṣudapāyo'nughāsam//

of Bhagavān. Emotional devotion is rooted in an experience of the nonduality of all things in Bhagavān, just as the conservative devotion is. Devotion as a goal is also equated with realization of the Supreme Lord.

These passages bring to mind the *Bhakti Sūtras* of Nārada, which are probably contemporary with, though not dependent upon, the *Bhāgavata*. The *Sūtras* are in the tradition of emotional devotion. For instance, Nārada defines devotion: "This, indeed, has the form of supreme love for him."[14] The word 'form' suggests that 'love' is here used analogously. Yet the devotion is emotional: "Knowing this love, a human is intoxicated, fixated, delighting in the Self. This love is not lust (*kāma*), since it is essentially a renunciation."[15] This is consistent with what we have seen in the *Bhāgavata* where devotion is closely associated in many passages with knowledge and forms of ascesis. Further devotion is a form of detachment (*nirodha*): "But Nārada holds that it is the dedication of every action to God and extreme anguish at forgetting him."[16]

Finally the *Sūtras* state: "There have been examples of this kind of love, namely, the cowherd girls of Vraja."[17] These girls are also the devotees par excellence for the *Bhāgavata* and its most significant example of the use of erotic love-symbolism.

The Ecstatic Play (*rāsalīlā*)

Canto ten recounts the biography of Kṛṣṇa, whose main mission is to rid the country of the tyrant demon Kaṃsa, who has usurped the throne of Mathurā from Kṛṣṇa's grandfather, Ugrasena. At his birth Kṛṣṇa, in order to escape Kaṃsa's wrath, is brought after several miraculous interventions to Vraja and raised by his foster parents, Nanda and Yaśodā. The prince is

14. *Aphorisms on the Gospel of Divine Love or Nārada Bhakti Sūtras*, translated by Swāmī Tyāgīśānanda (Mylapore, Madras: Sri Ramakrishna Math, 1972), p. 1, sūtra 2: sā tvasmin parapremarūpā/

15. *Ibid.*, p. 3, sūtras 6-7 : yat jñātvā matto bhavati stabdho bhavati ātmārāmo bhavati/ sā na kāmayamānā nirodharūpatvāt/

16. *Ibid.*, p. 7, sūtra 19 : nāradastu tadarpitākhilācāratā tadvismaraṇe paramavyākulateti/

17. *Ibid.*, sūtras 20-21 : astyevamevam/ yathā vrajagopikānām/

brought among cowherds, who came to love him more than their own children. After many miraculous exploits, when Kṛṣṇa was twelve, the ecstatic play (*rāsalīlā*) takes place (X.29-33). The young cowherd girls of the town (*gopī*) had all fallen in love and became infatuated with the beautiful and youthful Kṛṣṇa. They take a vow and adore the goddess Kātyāyanī with the prayer: "O goddess Kātyāyanī, the great creative energy (*māyā*), great yoginī, Supreme Ruler, praise to you, make the son of Nanda the cowherd, O goddess, my husband."[18] Each cowherd girl said this prayer and worshipped her. Their prayer is answered and Kṛṣṇa agrees to meet them on a night in autumn.

On a bright autumnal night, when the moon was full, Kṛṣṇa began to play melodies on his flute. All the cowherd girls are enraptured by its beautiful sound and flock to the woods outside of Vṛndāvana to find their beloved Kṛṣṇa. They dropped what they were doing, milking cows, cooking, serving their husbands, etc. "Being stopped by husbands, fathers, brothers, and relatives, with their minds lured and deluded by Govinda, they did not turn back."[19] Some of the cowherd girls were unable to get away. These practiced the devotion of separation. "By means of the unbearable and intense separation from their beloved their sins were shaken off and the beatitude of embracing Acyuta was achieved in contemplation."[20] These women were thus loosed from the bonds of their inherited destiny (*karma*) and freed from their bodies at that moment, even though "they recognized the Highest Self only as a paramour."[21] These women were unaware that Kṛṣṇa was Bhagavān or Brahman. They knew him only as an irresistible but illicit lover.

18. X.22.4 : kātyāyani mahāmāye mahāyoginyadhīśvari/ nandagopasutaṃ devi patiṃ me kuru te namaḥ/

19. X.29.8 : tā vāryamāṇāḥ patibhiḥ pitṛbhirbhrātṛbandhubhiḥ/ govindāpahṛtātmāno na nyavartanta mohitāḥ// Cf. *Harivaṃśa* LXIII.24: tā vāryamāṇāḥ pitṛbhir bhrātṛbhir mātṛbhis tathā/ kṛṣṇaṃ gopāṅganā rātrau mṛgayanti ratipriyāḥ// "Though prevented by their fathers and brothers and mothers, as well, the women of the Gopas, intent on making love, searched for Kṛṣṇa : in the dead of night." Translated by J. L. Masson, "The Childhood of Kṛṣṇa: Some Psychoanalytic Observations," *Journal of the Oriental Society*, XCIV (1974), 458.

20. X.29.10 : duḥsahapreṣṭhavirahatīvratāpadhutāśubhāḥ/ dhyānaprāptācyutāśleṣanirvṛtyā kṣīṇamaṅgalāḥ//

21. X.29.11a : tameva paramātmānaṃ jārabuddhyāpi saṃgatāḥ/

As the girls gather around him, Kṛṣṇa asks those who were able to come what it is they want and suggests that they return to their husbands, children and families since adultery is unvirtuous. Besides, as Kṛṣṇa cautions, "affection is from hearing, seeing, meditating, and singing, not from proximity, so return home."[22] Here Kṛṣṇa tells them to follow the ordinary ways of devotion. The cowherd girls, however, are saddened that perhaps Kṛṣṇa has no love for them. They plead with him: "As you, the knower of the religious law (*dharma*), have said, the natural duty of women is to give service to their husband, children, and relatives, O beloved one; let such service be done for you, the Lord, the theme of all teachings, the beloved friend, the Self of all embodied beings."[23] They want to substitute Kṛṣṇa for their husbands, bypassing the moral law by an appeal to the maker of the law. "Extinguish with the flood of nectar from your lips the fire of passion kindled by your smiles, glances, and music; if not, with our bodies consumed by the fire of separation by meditation, we shall attain to the position of your feet."[24]

Kṛṣṇa out of compassion consents to their wishes. The group proceeds to frolic on the banks of the Yamunā River, singing songs and playing, though hardly innocently: "Inflaming the passion of the charming women of Vraja by stretching his arms, embracing them, touching their hands, hair, thighs, waists, breasts, joking with them, and pressing his nails into their skin, with sportful glances and smiles, the Lord of love gave them sexual delight."[25] Yet the cowherd women grew conceited from

22. X.29.27: śravaṇāddarśanāddhyānānmayi bhāvo'nukīrtanāt/ na tathā saṃnikarṣeṇa pratiyāta tato gṛhān//

23. X.29.32 : yatpatyapatyasuhṛdāmanuvṛttiraṅga strīṇāṃ svadharma iti dharmavidā tvayoktam/ astvevametadupadeśapade tvayīśe preṣṭho bhavāṃstanubhṛtāṃ kila bandhurātmā//

24. X.29.35 : siñcāṅga nastvadadharāmṛtapūrakena hāsāvalokakalagītajahṛcchayāgnim/ no cedvayaṃ virahajāgnyupayuktadehā dhyānena yāma padayoḥ padavīṃ sakhe te//

25. X.29.46 : bāhuprasāraparirambhakarālakorunīvīstanālabhananarmanakhāgrapātaiḥ/kṣvelyā'valokahasitairvrajasundarīṇāmuttambhayanratipatiṃ ramayāṃcakāra// Cf. *Harivaṃśa* LXVII.23 : tās taṃ payodharottānair urobhiḥ samapīḍayan/ bhrāmitākṣaiś ca vadanair nirīkṣante varāṅganāḥ// "The girls pressed up close against him with their high firm breasts and their thighs, and with their whole face, the eyes rolling in ecstasy, they gazed at him."

their association with the passionate Kṛṣṇa. Therefore he disappeared from their midst in order to curb their pride and to provide a further occasion to shower grace upon them.

The cowherd women experienced all the agonies of separation from their beloved. Their response was to recall his presence. They imitate his gestures, sing his praises, and anxiously search for him. They remember and act of each of his exploits. Finding Kṛṣṇa's footsteps in his forest, they are hurt to discover that Kṛṣṇa has a companion in his flight: "Though delighting within his Self and sporting within his Self and unaffected, he sported with her, illustrating the wretchedness of the lovestricken and the wickedness of women."[26] The chosen cowherd girl in her turn becomes proud because of her exclusive possession of Kṛṣṇa, so he disappears from her too. All the cowherd girls now wander in the forest together. Not finding Kṛṣṇa, they sing his praises: "Give us, O heroic Lord, the nectar of your lips which increases enjoyment and destroys grief, which was fully enjoyed by the flute you sounded, and which makes people forget other attachments."[27] Suddenly Kṛṣṇa appears in their midst and the cowherd women, excited, flock around him: "The Lord took them to the bank of the Kālindī, where swarmed blackbees attracted by the gentle breeze charged with the fragrance of fully blossomed jasmines and Mandāras; the darkness of evening had been scattered by the abundant rays of the autumn moon; the spot was delightful, the soft sands spread like waves by the waves of the Kṛṣṇā."[28] Their heartache was now dissipated by the thrill of seeing him. They achieved their heart's desire when Kṛṣṇā made love to them.

Having made love with each of the cowherd girls, Kṛṣṇa started the ecstatic dance (*rāsa*) :[29] "Now commenced the start

26. X.30.34 : reme tayā cātmarata ātmārāmo'pyakhaṇḍitaḥ/kāmināṃ darśayandainyaṃ strīṇāṃ caiva durātmatām//

27. X.31.14 : suratavardhanaṃ śokanāśanaṃ svaritaveṇunā suṣṭhu cumbitam/ itararāgavismāraṇaṃ nṛṇāṃ vitara vīra naste'dharāmṛtam//

28. X.32.11-12 : tāḥ samādāya kālindyā nirviśya pulinaṃ vibhuḥ/ vikasatkundamandārasurabhyanilaṣaṭpadam// śaraccandrāṃśusaṃdohadhvastadoṣātamaḥ śivam/ kṛṣṇāyā hastataralācitakomalavālukam//

29. Cf. *Harivaṃśa* LXIII.25 : tās tu paṅktīkṛtāḥ sarvā ramayanti manoramam/gāyantyaḥ kṛṣṇacaritaṃ dvaṃdvaśo gopakanyakāḥ// "They all formed a circle around Kṛṣṇa and satisfied that beautiful boy, singing of his deeds in pairs."

of the ecstatic dance adorned with a circle of the cowherd girls, who stood with their necks encircled by Kṛṣṇa, the Lord of yogins, who placed himself between every two women, and whom each woman imagined to be at her side."[30] The cowherd women and Kṛṣṇa, who had multiplied himself, dance and sing as the court of heavenly beings looks on the marvels. "Thus by embracing, touching, casting loving glances, making amorous gestures, and laughing heartily, the Lord of Ramā, sported with the lovely women of Vraja, just as an infant plays with its reflections (in a mirror)."[31] The *Bhāgavata* is in awe of a Supreme Being who condescends to make love with such lowly women. "He placed himself in as many forms as there were cowherd women and although he was Bhagavān and delighted in himself, he made love to them from sport."[32] Then the dance ended and each of the cowherd women returned to her home, where she had not been missed, since through his creative energy Kṛṣṇa had made each husband think that his wife was actually at home with him all the time.

30. X.33.3: rāsotsavaḥ saṃpravṛtto gopīmaṇḍalamaṇḍitaḥ/ yogeśvareṇa kṛṣṇena tāsāṃ madhye dvayordvayoḥ/ praviṣṭena gṛhītānāṃ kaṇṭhe svanikaṭaṃ striyaḥ// Cf. *Viṣṇu Purāṇa* V. 13.49-52 : rāsamaṇḍalabandho'pi kṛṣṇapārśvamanujjñatā/gopījanena naivābhūdekasthānasthirātmanā// hastena gṛhya caikaikāṃ gopīnāṃ rāsamaṇḍalam/ cakāra tatkarasparśanimīlitadṛśaṃ hariḥ//tataḥ pravṛtto rāsaścaladvalayaniḥsvanaḥ/anuyātaśaratkāvyage yagītiranu kramāt// kṛṣṇaśśaraccandramasaṃ kaumudīṃ kumudākaram/ jagaugopīja nastvekaṃ kṛṣṇanāma punaḥ punaḥ/ "As each of the damsels attempted to remain in one place close to the side of Krishna, the circle of the dance could not be constructed. Thereupon taking each by the hand and when their eyelids were closed by the effects of such touch Hari formed the circle. Then began the dance in accompaniment with the music of their clashing bracelets and songs that celebrated in sweet melody the beauty of the autumnal season. Krishna sang the moon of autumn, a mine of gentle rays but the damsels chanted the praise of Krishna only." Translated by Manmatha Nath Dutt, *Prose English Translation of Vishnupuranam*, The Chowkhamba Sanskrit Studies, Vol. CX (Varanasi : Chowkhamba Sanskrit Series Office, 1972), p. 355.

31. X.33.17 : evaṃ pariṣvaṅgakarābhimarśasnigdhekṣaṇoddāmavilāsahāsaiḥ/ reme rameśo vrajasundarībhiryathārbhakaḥ svapratibimbavibhramaḥ//

32. X.33,20 : kṛtvā tāvantamātmānaṃ yāvatīrgopayoṣitaḥ/ reme sa bhagavāṃstābhirātmārāmo'pi līlayā//

Allegory and Eroticism

What we have here in the ecstatic play (*rāsalīlā*) of Kṛṣṇa with the cowherd women is an extremely complex story which can be understood on several levels. The story was scandalous to many Vaiṣṇavas. The redactor of the *Bhāgavata* apparently shared that scandal, though certainly not enough to suppress the story. His ambivalence is expressed through the comments that Śuka and Parīkṣit made during the narration of the story, where rationalizations are made for Kṛṣṇa's behaviour in committing adultery with the cowherd women. These comments are not present in the version of the ecstatic dance in the *Viṣṇu Purāṇa*. The story in the *Bhāgavata* was intended to be taken as an allegory at least at a certain level of understanding. Yet all Kṛṣṇa's exploits are interpreted allegorically in certain contexts. But this is not the only level of interpretation since the redactor was in awe of his subject matter and did not bowdlerize the story. In fact in comparison to the earlier accounts, the *Bhāgavata*'s account is embellished.[33] The fact that the radactor did not bowdlerize the story shows that for him the story has a certain historicity. The exploits of Kṛṣṇa, particularly the ecstatic play, are multivalent and the redactor preserved as many facets of their meaning that he could, although in doing this, he sacrificed a certain amount of consistency.

The eroticism of the *Bhāgavata*'s account of the ecstatic play is patent. The description is not one of a devotee whose experiences are only analogous to those of sexual bliss. The description is of explicitly erotic deeds. In several passages the *Bhāgavata* asserts that the *kāma* of the cowherd girls can be a liberating form of devotion.[34] *Kāma* is a strong term meaning 'concupiscence' or 'sexual desire.' The desire for Kṛṣṇa physically centered their attention on him to the exclusion of all else. Thus they surrendered themselves completely to him. Yet their love is scandalous on two levels since it was adulterous and compounded by the fact that they were not excused by the fact that he was a God. They were not even aware of his divine nature. As Kṛṣṇa

33. See Hardy's analysis of the relationship of the *Bhāgavata* to the Āḷvārs and to the *Viṣṇu Purāṇa* in *Viraha Bhakti*, p. 497-527.

34. Cf. VII.1.29b-30a.

says in the eleventh canto: "With sexual desire for me, thinking me as their lover, their paramour, the women by the hundreds and thousands, who did not know my true form, attained contact with me, the Highest Brahman."[35] Similarly Parīkṣit says that the cowherd women "knew Kṛṣṇa only as a lover, not as Brahman."[36] To which Śuka replies that the appearance of Bhagavān, "who is free from modification and unknowable and beyond the qualities, the Self of the qualities, is for the purpose of the final beatitude of people."[37] Bhagavān enters the sphere of the qualities so that those immersed in them might be saved by that manifestation of him from within the qualities. There is no one more immersed in the qualities than someone like the cowherd girl who is motivated by sexual desire. Thus sexual desire for Bhagavān frees one from sexual desire.

In chapter forty-seven of canto ten Kṛṣṇa sends Uddhava as an emissary to the cowherd women. One of them then sang the 'bee song' for him: "Having allowed us to drink from his lips but once, he left us distraught, just as a bee like you would leave a flower."[38] She expresses the sentiments of a cast-off mistress. Uddhava is struck by the poignancy of this situation: "These two are strange, the wandering of the women in the woods, sinning by infidelity, and their surpassing affection for Kṛṣṇa, the Highest Self; surely the Lord directly and freely confers beatitude on those who worship him unknowingly, just as the best drug, when consumed, heals."[39] The manifestation of Kṛṣṇa's adulterous love making with the cowherd women confounds the wisdom of the *Vedas* and of the traditional religious teaching. In this way the *Bhāgavata* tries on one level to deal with the facticity of the cowherd women's adulterous love for Kṛṣṇa.

35. XI.12.13 : matkāmā ramaṇaṃ jāramasvarūpavido'balāḥ/ brahma māṃ paramaṃ prāpuḥ saṅgācchatasahasraśaḥ//

36. X.29.12a : kṛṣṇaṃ viduḥ paraṃ kāntaṃ na tu brahmatayā mune/

37. X.29.14 : nṛṇāṃ niḥśreyasārthāya vyaktirbhagavato nṛpa/ avyayasyāprameyasya nirguṇasya guṇātmanaḥ//

38. X.47.13a : sakṛdadharasudhāṃ svāṃ mohinīṃ pāyayitvā sumanasa iva sadyastatyaje' smānbhavādṛk/

39. X.47.59 : kvemāḥ striyo vanacarīrvyabhicāraduṣṭāḥ kṛṣṇe kva caiṣa paramātmani rūḍhabhāvaḥ/ nanvīśvaro 'nubhajato'viduṣo'pi sākṣācchreyastanotyagadarāja ivopayuktaḥ//

In the face of the indignation of the righteous, the *Bhāgavata* maintains the force of the story. Love for Kṛṣṇa in any way, especially in this way, saves since the essence of devotion is love for Bhagavān.

However, the *Bhāgavata* also accepts the injunctions against promiscuity and the general teaching of the Law Books (*dharma śāstras*) that sexuality binds the indulger to the cycle of death and rebirth. In canto three Kapila tells Devahūti that the "bondage and infatuation which arise from attachment to any other object are not so complete as that from the attachment of a man to a woman."[40] Woman is a form of delusion which conquers a man merely by the movement of an eyebrow. "The woman who slowly entraps is the creative energy (*māyā*) of God; one must regard her as the death of the self, like a well covered with grass."[41] The context here is one where the rules of Yoga and the discipline of devotion (*bhaktiyoga*) are being described and the behavior prescribed is what would be expected of a yogin. The *Bhāgavata* is not recommending Tantric practices. The bondage and infatuations produced by the creative energy can be overcome by the discipline of devotion since they have only a relative reality. The bondage and infatuations of the cowherd girls, though they are immersed in the realm of the constituent qualities, are directed to the absolutely real, who is present for his own sport in Vṛndāvana as Bhagavān Kṛṣṇa.

We have already seen that those cowherd girls who were unable to go to the forest tryst with Kṛṣṇa were able to contemplate his form with loving devotion within their minds and in that way achieve liberation.[42] Indeed Kṛṣṇa praises the cowherd girls for coming to him, motivated as they were by desire : "Because your minds are bound to me by attachment, you may have come; it is proper for you because all creatures delight in me."[43] In either case, the interior attitude is what constitutes

40. III.31.35 : na tathā'sya bhavenmoho bandhaścānyaprasaṅgataḥ/ yoṣitsaṅgādyathā puṃso yathā tatsaṅgisaṅgataḥ//

41. III.31.40 : yopayāti śanairmāyā yoṣiddevavinirmitā/ tāmīkṣetātmano mṛtyuṃ tṛṇaiḥ kūpamivāvṛtam// Cf. XI.14.29-30.

42. Cf. X.29.10-11.

43. X.29.23 : athavā madabhisnehādbhavatyo yantritāśayāḥ/ āgatā hyupapannaṃ vaḥ prīyante mayi jantavaḥ//

devotion. Thus to the cowherd girls who came to him in the forest he recommends that they return to their homes since their desire is sufficient: "The intercourse with an illicit lover by women of good family is everywhere a horrible deed, fraught with fear, wicked, unprofitable, scandalous, and a bar to heaven."[44] Yet the cowherd girls persist: "What woman of the three worlds would not deviate from virtuous conduct, bewitched by your flute's music with its mellifluous sound and melodious tunes; having gazed on this form, the most graceful in the three worlds, even cows, birds, trees, and animals get a thrill of joy."[45] Such appeals take heaven by storm, and Kṛṣṇa out of compassion decides to give them delight in the ecstatic play, in which he makes love to them and sports in the *rāsa* dance. Their persistent yearning for Kṛṣṇa saved the cowherd girls. Indeed they were rewarded with the highest kind of bliss.

However, the *Bhāgavata* on another level offers some explanation for this adulterous behavior of its Supreme Deity. Parīkṣit asks Śuka how it was that Kṛṣṇa who came to the earth in order to establish virtue (*dharma*) and suppress sin could commit a transgression by making love to the wives of other men: "O Holy Sage, with what intent did the Lord of the Yadus, who had all his desires satisfied, commit so horrible a deed?"[46] Śuka in reply suggests that there are two standards. Religious duty (*dharma*) indeed is in force for ordinary humans, but for the Lord there is a higher standard: "A precept of the mighty is true, but their conduct not necessarily; the intelligent man should follow only what is consistent with their precepts."[47] There cannot be any bondage for the Lord since he became a person of his own free will. Those who are devoted to him are not bound, nor those who have released their inherited destiny

44. X.29.26 : asvargyamayaśasyaṃ ca phalgu kṛcchraṃ bhayāvaham/ jugupsitaṃ ca sarvatra aupapatyaṃ kulastriyāḥ//

45. X.29.40 : kā stryaṅga te kalapadāyatamūrcchitena saṃmohitārya-caritānna calettrilokyām/ trailokyasaubhagamidaṃ ca nirīkṣya rūpaṃ yadgodvijadrumamṛgāḥ pulakānyabibhran//

46. X.33.29 : āptakāmo yadupatiḥ kṛtavānvai jugupsitam/ kimabhiprāya etaṃ naḥ saṃśayaṃ chindhi suvrata//

47. X.33.32 : īśvarāṇāṃ vacaḥ satyaṃ tathaivācaritaṃ kvacit/ teṣāṃ yatsvavacoyuktaṃ buddhimāṃstatsamācaret//

(*karma*) by means of Yoga, how then can he who has done these things for his devotee be bound? Śuka suggests that one should do what Bhagavān says not what he does. Someone, especially the Supreme Lord, who has been liberated and thus is not subject to his inherited destiny is not subject to the precepts of the religious law. Bhagavān cannot be bound by the law which he has made, although it still binds men. In other words, Kṛṣṇa's actions, no matter how contrary they are to the religious law, cannot bind him who is its master to the death-rebirth cycle.

Śuka reenforces this rationale with one drawn from non-dualism. Kṛṣṇa "indwells the cowherd girls, their husbands, and all embodied beings, presides over them, and has assumed a body here for sport."[48] He assumes a body for the good of all beings and he sports with them so that when they hear about it they too will become devoted to him. These events have been narrated in order to inculcate devotion. Because Kṛṣṇa is Bhagavān there is an 'exemplar' causality by which his actions accomplish what they intend even from the mere hearing of them. There is an appropriate connection between the action and the sentiment which will arise when the action is heard of. Bhagavān appeared in the Dvāpara age in order to be a mainfest object for the devotion of the cowherd girls, who as simple women were devoted to him in a sexual manner. The *Bhāgavata Purāṇa* appears in the Kali age in order to enculcate devotion by telling Bhagavān's story: "He who full of faith hears in proper order, or recounts, the story of the sports of Viṣṇu with the women of Vraja is blessed with the highest devotion to Bhagavān, he masters his own heart before long and overcomes sexual desire."[49] Hearing of Kṛṣṇa's compassion for and satisfaction of the desire of the cowherd girls causes a sublimation of desire in the devotee. Just as for the cowherd girl desire (*kāma*) functions to center her body and soul on Kṛṣṇa, so for the latter-day

48. X.33.36 : gopīnāṃ tatpatīnāṃ ca sarveṣāmeva dehinām/ yo'ntaścarati so'dhyakṣaḥ krīḍaneneha dehabhāk//

49. X.33.40 : vikrīḍitaṃ vrajavadhūbhiridaṃ ca viṣṇoḥ śraddhānvito' nusṛṇuyādatha varṇayedyaḥ/ bhaktiṃ parāṃ bhagavati pratilabhya kāmaṃ hṛdrogamāśvapahinotyacireṇa dhīraḥ//

devotee hearing about the cowherd girl's love for Kṛṣṇa helps him to cast aside desire, which is distracting him, and so focus his mind exclusively on Bhagavān Kṛṣṇa.

The *Bhāgavata* in its multivalent understanding of the ecstatic play has taken it literally as historical, a real grace-full manifestation of Kṛṣṇa in the Dvāpara age, and then drawn a moral conclusion appropriate for the devotee in Kali age. Aside from this realistic interpretation, the *Bhāgavata* also suggests a symbolic interpretation, verging on allegory. From the start of the narration of the ecstatic play, the allegory is hinted at: "Glorious Bhagavān decided to sport, supported by his yogic energy (*yogamāyā*)."[50] Yogic energy here indicates that Vṛndāvana and all that happens there belong to a special realm wherein Bhagavān's majesty (*aiśvarya*), his sweetness (*madhura*), and his grace (*prasāda*) are revealed. To mention yogic energy here is equivalent to 'once upon a time.' Again throughout the narration the titles and epithets suggest this allegorical meaning. For example: "Surrounded by the women, who had shaken off their sorrow, Bhagavān Acyuta shone brightly, like the Person with his powers (*śakti*)."[51] The cowherd women are similar to the powers of Bhagavān, which reveal his glories, make his purposes known, and display him in the forms of creation, the powers being the equivalent of the three qualities. All this is done without any diminution of Bhagavān's transcendence. It is not a great step to see Kṛṣṇa and the cowherd girls, who serve his play, as a symbol of Bhagavān surrounded by his created and creative powers.

The *Bhāgavata* is also conscious of its own uses of the standard poetical devices of Sanskrit literature. There is a hint that things should not be taken too literally, since its description of the erotic exuberances associated with the autumnal rites conforms to the standards of the poetic *rasas*, tastes or sentiments, which are the emotional postures of Sanskrit drama : "The truly desired one, who was loved by masses of women, and who made

50. X.29.1 : bhagavānapi tā rātrīḥ śaradotphullamallikāḥ/ vīkṣya rantuṃ manaścakre yogamāyāmupāśritaḥ//

51. X.32.10 : tābhirvidhūtaśokābhirbhagavānacyuto vṛtaḥ/ vyarocatādhikaṃ tāta puruṣaḥ śaktibhiryathā//

love though enclosed in himself, enjoyed sexually all those nights illuminated by the rays of the moon, exemplifying the emotions appropriate to poetic stories of autumn."[52] A god whose love-play conforms to the canons of poetic convention surely is intended to have some symbolical meaning. Here the ecstatic play is symbolic of the indescribable ecstasy which results whenever Bhagavān indulges in the enjoyment of his own Self for the sake of others, whom he has created for that very purpose. According to S. Bhaṭṭācārya the conventions were as follows:

> Such a union of Kṛṣṇa with the cowherd women represented the perfect revelation of the sentiment of love (*premarasa*), in which the nucleus (*ālambana*) was Kṛṣṇa, the exciting conditions (*uddīpana*) were the full moon, the fragrance of the flowers, etc., the expressive conditions (*anubhāva*) were the different gestures of the cowherd girls and the fluctuating conditions (*sañcāribhāva*) were pique, sorrow, etc. on the part of the *gopīs*.[53]

Thus Kṛṣṇa is the perfect revelation of the perfect bliss of Bhagavān. Each of the cowherd girls, by his grace, is able to embrace that bliss, according to her capacity, to its full. This is why the *Bhāgavata* describes Kṛṣṇa as appearing separately for each girl in the dancing circle. The wild dance itself is the expression of the abandon and self-forgetfulness connected with the ecstasy of devotion to Kṛṣṇa. The circle has no beginning and no end. When one enters the divine bliss, it goes on forever. Since ecstasy is beyond description, the *Bhāgavata* gives in these passages an allegorical interpretation to the ecstatic play.

Separation

In searching for the import of the *Bhāgavata*'s ecstatic play, one cannot limit oneself only to the five chapters which describe it since the story of Kṛṣṇa's dalliance with the cowherd girls has a sequel. The ecstatic play is the Indian summer of Kṛṣṇa's youth. Immediately afterwards he must go to Mathurā in order to overthrow the tyrant Kaṃsa. He never returns to Vṛndāvana. Kṛṣṇa

52. X.33.26: evaṃ śaśāṅkāṃśuvirājitā niśāḥ sa satyakāmo'nuratābalāgaṇaḥ/ siṣeva ātmanyavaruddhasauratah sarvāḥ śaratkāvyakathārasāśrayāḥ//
53. Bhaṭṭācārya, *The Philosophy of the Śrīmad-Bhāgavata*, I. 127-28.

later marries Rukmiṇī, Jāmbavatī, Satyabhāmā, and sixteen thousand others, and forgets the cowherd girls of Vraja. But they do not forget him, since in Vṛndāvana they continually tell stories of him and sing his praises : "Recalling again and again the actions of their dear one during his infancy and boyhood, they sang and wept, having forgotten shame."[54] When Uddhava came to Vṛndāvana as Kṛṣṇa's emissary, one of the cowherd girls sang the 'bee song' to him. Its main theme is the pains and anguish of their separation from Kṛṣṇa, upon which Uddhava commented that "due to your separation you have developed a great affection for Adhokṣaja, thus you have given a great grace to me by giving me a glimpse of your ardent devotion."[55] Their separation from Kṛṣṇa has increased their devotion to him to a greater pitch than when he was present before their eyes. Uddhava then conveys a special message for them from Kṛṣṇa: "Your separation from me, the Self of all, is not really possible; just as the elements, ether, air, fire, water and earth are in beings, I abide as the support of mind, the vital airs, the elements, senses, and the qualities."[56] Ultimately there can be no separation at all between Kṛṣṇa and the cowherd girls since Kṛṣṇa is present to them as their Self and as the support of the world they live in. On the phenomenal level, however, Kṛṣṇa keeps away from the cowherd girls in order to increase their devotion : "It is only for the sake of focusing your mind constantly on me while you eagerly meditate on me that I, your beloved, stay so far from your sight."[57] Separation is superior to proximity, which diverts the mind from the purpose of devotion: "The mind of women does not get so absorbed in the thought of their beloved who is close by and before their eyes as by his staying far away."[58]

54. X.47.10 : gāyantyaḥ priyakarmāṇi rudatyaśca gatahriyaḥ/ tasya saṃsmṛtya saṃsmṛtya yāni kaiśorabālyayoḥ //

55. X.47.27 : sarvātmabhāvo'dhikṛto bhavatīnāmadhokṣaje/ viraheṇa mahābhāgā mahānme'nugrahaḥ kṛtaḥ //

56. X.47.29 : bhavatīnāṃ viyogo me nahi sarvātmanā kvacit/ yathā bhūtāni bhūteṣu khaṃ vāyvagnirjalaṃ mahī/ tathāhaṃ ca manaḥprāṇabhūtendriyaguṇāśrayaḥ//

57. X.47.34 : yattvahaṃ bhavatīnāṃ vai dūre varte priyo dṛśām/ manasaḥ saṃnikarṣārthaṃ madanudhyānakāmyayā//

58. X.47.35 : yathā dūracare preṣṭhe mana āviśya vartate/ strīṇām ca na tathā cetaḥ saṃnikṛṣṭe'kṣagocare//

This theme of the separation of lovers is an ancient one in Sanskrit and Indian literature. In the *Mahābhārata* the story of Nala and Damayantī illustrates this sentiment. The ideal lover is better exemplified in a woman than in a man. The man is enmeshed in desire, sensuousness, and egoism. The Hindu wife is the ideal of conjugal fidelity, total devotion, and self-surrender, extending even to heroic sacrifice of self. The husband is the model of infidelity, which only better allows the wife to demonstrate her selfless devotion. This devotion of the wife for her husband has the character of religious ascesis. Thus Ch. Vaudeville remarks:

> The Indian Epic, therefore, knows *preman* as an ideal love-relationship between husband and wife, rising above mere sensual desire, *kāma*. But it is the wife, and she alone, who is really transformed and elevated by it, and who makes it, so to speak, her own *sādhana*. The pure Hindu wife, the Satī, is already a type of *Bhakta*.[59]

Several centuries later, in the *Bhāgavata*, this theme of separation (*viraha*) is transferred to the adulterous cowherd girls, who risk the scorn of the righteous, to delight in Kṛṣṇa, and yet they must surrender their bliss in him for the agony of separation. Thus Vaudeville continues :

> Though *parakīya* [adulterous] according to the letter, the Gopis are *svakīya*, faithful and chaste wives, according to the spirit, in so far as they serve to typify the highest form of *Bhakti*, which is conceived as a sorrowful yearning for the presence and the vision of Kṛṣṇa.[60]

The interior yearning which accompanies separation is the highest form of devotion. Nārada in his *Bhakti Sūtras* gives separation first place.[61] An early Vaiṣṇava theologian, Yāmunācārya, conceived devotion in this way : "Vision is high devotion; union is high knowledge; fear of new separation is the highest devo-

59. Vaudeville, "Evolution of Love-Symbolism in Bhagavatism," p. 33.
60. *Ibid.*, p. 38.
61. *Nārada Bhakti Sūtras*, p. 27, sūtra 82.

tion."[62] Devotion is thus dynamic, a tension rather than the rest of repose in bliss. Even in possession it is an unquenchable thirst, like the intense sexual desire of an illicit love affair. In this sense, Uddhava tells the cowherd girls that they are to be congratulated that "the highest devotion to the renowned Bhagavān which is hard even for sages to attain has been attained by you."[63] And again : "I salute again and again the dust of the feet of the women of Nanda's Vraja, whose singing of Hari's stories purifies the three worlds."[64] The cowherd girls are the perfect devotees, the examples to emulate in their devotion to Kṛṣṇa: "What penance did the cowherd girls do that they drink with their eyes his dazzling form, the essence of beauty, which is not only unsurpassed but unequaled, not adorned by anything external, eternally new, hard to attain, the exclusive abode of renown, splendor, and majesty"[65]

This description of devotion is very different from the Yoga type of devotion described in the previous chapter. Rather than being 'without qualities,' this type of devotion is immersed in the qualities. Rather than seeking the bliss of the experience of union, it seeks and glories in the pangs of separation. In devotion without qualities the devotee melts his interior stream of consciousness into the pure, undifferentiated consciousness of Brahman. Denigrating the individuality and personality of the devotee, it endangers the uniqueness and personality of Bhagavān Kṛṣṇa. As if in recognition of this danger, the *Bhāgavata* compliments the devotion without qualities found in the discourses of the second, third, and eleventh cantos with the love (*preman*) devotion of the tenth canto. Love devotion with its corollary, separation (*viraha*) devotion, is confident enough in the essential non-duality of Bhagavān and the individual self to resist absorption of the individuality and personality of the indi-

62. Quoted in Tyāgīśānanda, *Aphorisms on the Gospel of Divine Love or Nārada Bhakti Sūtras*, p. 52; darśanaṃ parabhaktiḥ syāt parajñānaṃ tu saṅgamaḥ/ punarviśleṣabhīrutvam paramā bhaktirucyate//

63. X.47.25 : bhagavatyuttamaśloke bhavatībhiranuttamā/ bhaktiḥ pravartitā diṣṭyā munīnāmapi durlabhā//

64. X.47.63 : vande nandavrajastrīṇāṃ pādareṇumabhīkṣṇaśaḥ/ yāsāṃ harikathodgītaṃ punāti bhuvanatrayam//

65. X.44.14 : gopyastapaḥ kimacaranyadamuṣya rūpaṃ lāvaṇyasāramasamordhvamananyasiddham/ dṛgbhiḥ pibantyanusavābhinavaṃ durāpamekāntadhāma yaśasaḥ śriya aiśvarasya//

vidual devotee into an impersonal Brahman. The mystical pangs of the separation from Kṛṣṇa, after the bliss of union with him, parallels and reflects the metaphysical reality of the individual self within the external bliss, consciousness, and being of Bhagavān, whose supereminent love supports the separate existence of his lover-devotee. Thus both strands of the *Bhāgavata*'s devotion are grounded in non-dualism. Both allow the existence of the phenomenal world a place within that non-dualism. Yet the conservative devotion which stems from the *Bhagavad Gītā*, which is treated in the *Bhāgavata*'s discourses, emphasizes the transcendence of Bhagavān and the relative nothingness of his devotee. The innovative devotion, which is treated in the narratives of the tenth canto, projects an image of a Bhagavān who is incarnationally involved with his devotees. The one form of devotion reenforces the reality of Bhagavān, while the other confirms the reality of the devotee. The *Bhāgavata* thus in its total import ties both Bhagavān and his devotee together in a vision of a non-dualism with qualities (*saviśeṣādvaita*) from either of the two points of view.

Chapter VII

INTERPRETATIONS OF THE *BHĀGAVATA*

The unique place of the *Bhāgavata* in the devotional literature of India is shown by the plethora of commentaries upon it. The first literary reference to the *Bhāgavata* is found in Alberuni in 1030 A.D. Vopadeva (12th century) wrote the *Harilīlā*, an index to the *Bhāgavata*. As we have seen, there is no mention of the *Bhāgavata* in the corpus of Rāmānuja. Strangely two followers of Śaṃkara were the first to write commentaries, in a non-dualist vein, on the *Bhāgavata*, Citsukha (12th or 13th century) and Puṇyarāṇya (?). Apparently there were two wings to the school of Śaṃkara, a *Smārta* group who were followers of the path of knowledge and a *Bhāgavata* group who practiced devotion as a means to the realization of Brahman. These latter produced the commentaries, now lost. Madhva (1238-1317) answered this non-dualist interpretation in his *Bhāgavata Tātparya*. The famous Śrīdhara Svāmin wrote his commentary around 1325, apparently softening his non-dualist interpretation as a result of Madhva's commentary. Vallabha wrote his *Subodhinī* around 1500. The Caitanya School after 1500 produced many works on the *Bhāgavata*.

Madhva

Three theologies regard the *Bhāgavata* as authoritative: the dualist (*dvaita*) theology of Madhva, the pure non-dualist (*śuddhādvaita*) theology of Vallabha, and the ineffable difference-in-identity (*acintyabhedābheda*) theology of the Caitanya School. An investigation of these schools will shed light on the *Bhāgavata*'s original religious structure and the potentiality it had for development. Madhva was born around the beginning of the thirteenth century, at least three hundred years after the *Bhāgavata*'s final redaction. He founded a highly original system of dualism on the basis of the Vedāntic tradition. By dualism Madhva does not mean two independent and mutually irreducible substances, as does classical Sāṃkhya. If he had, he could hardly claim to follow the *Bhāgavata*. The use of the English term 'dualism' for *dvaita* must be nuanced to avoid misunderstanding Madhva's intention. According to Madhva there are three irreducible substances, but only one independent substance, God. The other two, the individual selves (*jīva*), and the material world (*jaḍa*), are dependent upon God.

Thus there is a dependent but eternal difference between God and the other realities, since God is the efficient but not the material cause of the universe. This according to Madhva corrects the illogical paradox of the qualified non-dualism (*viśiṣṭādvaita*) of Rāmānuja. Because of this difference, the bondage and liberation of the individual self are real, and not to be regarded as produced by a delusive energy (*māyā*). There are five eternal differences: between God and the individual self, between one individual self and another, between the individual self and the inanimate world, and between one inanimate object and another. God has an infinite number of qualities, although he remains always one. The selves are eternally different from God and go through a succession of existences, characterized by ignorance. The world is derived from primal nature (*prakṛti*), its material cause, a non-intelligent principle distinct from God. Liberation is the result of direct knowledge of Hari. The means to that knowledge are detachment, tranquility, self-surrender, devotion, etc. Even in the state of liberation, the individual self is distinct from God.

According to Madhva, the *Bhāgavata* has a place along with the *Upaniṣads*, the *Bhagavad Gītā*, and the *Brahma Sūtras* as authoritative Scriptures (*prasthāna*). In order to refute the doctrine of illusion (*māyā*) of Śaṃkara, which was considered to undermine the value of devotion and to deprecate the majesty of Bhagavān, Madhva searched these Scriptures for every evidence of difference between God and man. To those passages which showed a non-dualist tendency he gave a refutation and clarification. His *Bhāgavata Tātparya* contains 3600 sections, which comment upon some 1600 of the *Bhāgavata*'s 18,000 verses. He draws at times upon Pāñcarātra sources to augment his interpretation. He treats only the critical passages, which are open to non-dualist interpretation, especially those in the tenth and eleventh cantos.

Two passages of the *Bhāgavata* are central to Madhva's doctrine and quoted in his works. The first is from the second canto where Śuka says : "Matter, inherited destiny (*karma*), time, the innate essence of beings (*svabhāva*) and the individual selves exist only by his grace and cease to exist the moment he grows indifferent towards them."[1] Thus the existence of the individual selves, etc. are metaphysically dependent upon the will of God. Brahman is the only existent who is really independent, the controlling Supreme Spirit (*niyāmaka*). The second verse is from canto one where Nārada says : "This universe is indeed Bhagavān but in a way different; it is from him that there is the maintenance, destruction, and creation of the world."[2] This text gives Madhva a clue for the reconciliation of the texts which identify all things with Brahman with those texts which affirm the reality of the world, especially in his Commentary on the *Brahma Sūtras*.[3]

Again, Madhva picks out passages which recognize the distinctive existence of primal nature (*prakṛti*) which Śaṃkara, Nimbārka and Rāmānuja had asserted could not be based upon Scripture (*aśabdatvam*). For instance, in canto one Sūta says: "The supreme Bhagavān, who is without qualities, formerly created this universe by means of the creative energy of his Self, which consists of qualities and has the form of cause and effect (*sat-asat*)."[4] The Lord is distinct from primal nature. He is not the ultimate material cause. Yet he sets the evolution of primal nature in motion as its efficient cause. As distinct from Bhagavān, the world is real, yet it is unreal to the extent that it is dependent upon him.

The realization of the difference (*bhedajñāna*) between God, the individual selves, and the world constitutes a knowledge that saves. Madhva in his *Brahma Sūtra Bhāṣya* quotes a variant

1. II.10.12 : dravyaṃ karma ca kālaśca svabhāvo jīva eva ca/ yadanugrahataḥ santi na santi yadupekṣayā//

2. I.5.20a : idaṃ hi viśvaṃ bhagavānivetaro yato jagatsthānanirodhasaṃbhavāḥ/

3 Especially in reference to *Brahma Sūtras* I.1.17 : bhedavyapadeśācca/

4. I.2.30 : sa evedaṃ sasarjāgre bhagavānātmamāyayā/ sadasadrūpayā cāsau guṇamayyā' guṇo vibhuḥ//

reading in canto eleven of the *Bhāgavata* in support of his doctrine : "My state of lordship is fortune and the highest gain is devotion to me; wisdom consists in knowing (*bodha*) difference in the self and Hrī (modesty) is being on guard against actions."[5] What Madhva is doing in these texts is interpreting certain passages in the light of other passages. The identity or non-duality texts are subordinated to difference texts. The literal sense sometimes stands in the way of the true meaning: "Texts proclaiming identity between the individual self and Brahman admit of other reasonable interpretations in terms of the metaphysical independence and primacy of the Supreme, identity of place or interest, similarity of attributes and so on."[6] His main concern seems to be to preserve and respect the majesty and supremacy of Viṣṇu. Identity texts can be interpreted in terms of mystical union. In a conflict between an identity text and a difference text, the identity text can be subordinated to the difference text. In this case Viṣṇu's supremacy would be preserved but not vice versa, unless one introduced a principle of illusion or ignorance, but illusion would mar that supremacy. Thus Madhva states that

> the difference texts do not admit of any other explanation; they would keep their vantage; the theory of unreal difference stands refuted on account of the untenability of ignorance obscuring Brahman. For when Brahman that is by definition devoid of *viśeṣas* (attributes) shines in self-luminosity, there is nothing in it that could be deceived by ignorance. The assumption of unreal aspects in it, to render the work of ignorance intelligible, would again presuppose the presence of an earlier ignorance.[7]

5. XI.19.40: bhago ma aiśvaro bhāvo lābho madbhaktiruttamaḥ/ vidyātmani bhidābādho jugupsā hrīrakarmasu// Cf. B. N. K. Sharma, *A History of the Dvaita School of Vedānta and Its Literature* (Bombay: Bookseller's Publishing Co., 1960), I, 172. Instead of *bhidābādho*, removing difference, Madhva reads *bhidābodhaḥ*, knowing difference.

6. *Anuvyākhyāna*: svātantraye ca viśiṣṭatve sthānamatyaikyayorapi/ sādṛśye caikyavāk samyak sāvakāśā yatheṣṭataḥ// Quoted and translated by B. N. K. Sharma, *Madhva's Teaching in His Own Words* (Bombay: Bharatiya Vidya Bhavan, (1970), p. 64.

7. *Anuvyākhyāna* : avakāśojjñatā bhedaśrutirnātibalā katham/ ajñānāsaṃbhavādeva mithyābhedo nirākṛtaḥ/ nirviśeṣe svayaṃbhāte kimajñānāvṛtaṃ bhavet/ mithyāviśeṣo'pyajñānasiddhimeva hyapekṣate/ *Ibid.*, p. 65.

In other words, difference texts cannot be explained away since there cannot be a veil of ignorance spread over Brahman. Difference makes the Scriptures, including the *Bhāgavata*, intelligible.

Madhva emphasizes the *Bhāgavata*'s conservative, meditative devotion, which he defines as "the attachment of the heart towards him, preceded by a full knowledge and belief that he is the best thing."[8] And again, "the firm and unshakable love of God, which rises above all other ties of love and affection based upon an adequate knowledge and conviction of his great majesty."[9] That knowledge carries the conviction of one's dependent reality and of Bhagavān's independent reality. Knowledge and devotion are not in conflict but coalesce. The knowledge of difference makes sense of liberation. There must be a difference between the devotee and Bhagavān. For Madhva this religious imperative becomes metaphysical. That which is different in the world must be different in liberation. This is the profoundest insight of devotion.

However, Madhva does not base his system solely on the *Bhāgavata*. His hermeneutical presuppositions in favor of difference texts, based on his insight into the dynamic of devotion, allows him to broaden the basis of Vedānta to include the *Vedas*, the Pāñcarātra literature, and the *Purāṇas* like the *Bhāgavata*. With this broadened base he constructs a system whose foundation is the majesty of Viṣṇu, upon whom everything else is dependent. He derives much of his teaching from the Pāñcarātra. Thus he allows a place for Lakṣmī as the consort of Viṣṇu, although he allows no place for the presiding manifestations (*vyūha*) of Bhagavān. In addition the romantic element of the Kṛṣṇa manifestation along with both the cowherd girls and Rādhā is downplayed so Madhva can disallow the *Bhāgavata*'s emotional devotion. Madhva was thoroughly in command of his scriptural authorities and not a slave to their literal sense. He perhaps preserves some of the intention of the *Bhāgavata*'s redactor by

8. *Bhāṣya on Bṛhadāraṇyaka Upaniṣad* I.4, quoted in A. K. Lad, *A Comparative Study of the Concept of Liberation in Indian Philosophy* (Chowk: Girharlal Keshavdas, 1967), p. 162.

9. *Ibid.*

his stress on the absolute supremacy of Bhagavān Viṣṇu, the absolute need for the grace of Viṣṇu for emancipation, and the eternal dependent separation of the individual self from Bhagavān. He neglects or ignores the strong Kṛṣṇa element in the *Bhāgavata*. While his interpretation of the identity, non-dualist, texts of the *Bhāgavata* is consistent with his interpretation of their roots in the Upaniṣadic identity texts, this interpretation would seem to be the literal sense neither in the *Bhāgavata* nor in the *Upaniṣads*. This, however, is not to fault Madhva since texts never stand alone, but are always in need of and subject to interpretation. The canons of a critical redaction analysis are not those of Hindu theologians.

Vallabha

The pure non-dualism (*śuddhādvaita*) or the path of grace (*puṣṭimārga*) of Vallabha (1479-1531) is derived directly from the *Bhāgavata*. H. V. Glasenapp characterizes Vallabha's doctrine as "a systematization of the *Bhāgavata Purāṇa* in the light of certain epistemological views and sectarian ideas."[10] According to Vallabha Scripture is the only valid means of knowing Brahman. The other means are valid only to the extent that they conform to Scripture. The *Bhāgavata* is the fourth authoritative Scripture (*prasthāna*), which removes all the doubts and uncertainties raised in the three previous Scriptures, the *Vedas*, and *Bhagavad Gītā*, and the *Brahma Sūtras*. It is the final court of appeal for Vallabha. In his *Commentary* on the *Brahma Sūtras* Vallabha often cites the *Bhāgavata* rather than the *Upaniṣads* to support his position. In the third section of the *Tattvārtha Dīpa Nibandha*, the *Bhāgavatārtha*, Vallabha considers the general themes of the *Bhāgavata* and in the *Subodhinī* he gives a verse commentary for the first three cantos, a part of the fourth, the tenth, and a part of the eleventh.

On account of his complete antagonism to Śaṃkara's doctrine of *māyā*, Vallabha's system is designated pure non-dualism

10. "Die Lehre Vallabhācārya," *Zeitschrift für Indologie und Iranistik*, Bd. IX (1934), quoted in Mrudula Marfatia, *The Philosophy of Vallabhācārya* (Delhi : Munshiram Manoharlal, 1967), p. 43.

(*śuddhādvaita*), non-dualism which is untainted by the dualism of an illusion-causing *māyā*. His non-dualism is uncompromising: reality is one, Brahman is Bhagavān Kṛṣṇa and all-pervading. Everything that exists in the world is Brahman, there is no second. Brahman is the cause and the effect. When Bhagavān suppresses or obscures (*tirobhāva*) his quality of bliss (*ānanda*), the world appears. When he reveals his bliss (*āvirbhāva*), the world becomes pure Brahman. This process occurs for his sport, by his own free will, subject to no compulsion of illusion (*māyā*). Brahman evolves the world from himself by suppressing some of his attributes. Difference is only a state of being an effect. It does not exist within the cause. Thus the world and the individual selves in it are Brahman, qualified by nothing other than his own pleasure. Vallabha follows the *Bhāgavata*'s use of the term *māyā*. It is the creative energy of Bhagavān by which he assumes the forms of all existent beings.[11] The world and the selves are existent potentially or latently within Bhagavān, who is the material (*upādāna*), efficient (*nimitta*), and inherent (*samavāyi*) causes. The inherent cause is Bhagavān's actual, inseparable, and continuous presence in the world and in the individual selves. He is present in his effects and one (*tādātmya*) with them. Thus pure non-dualism means that everything is Brahman, one without a second, in contrast to Śaṃkara's absolute non-dualism (*kevalādvaita*) where Brahman is the only reality, everything else being unreal due to illusion (*māyā*). Bhagavān is therefore the support of opposing qualities and is manifest in multiple forms.

Brahman has three forms: (1) the highest is the divine (*ādhidaivika*) form, Kṛṣṇa or the Highest Person; (2) the impersonal (*akṣara*) form in which the attributes of being, knowledge, and bliss are unmanifest; and (3) the inner controller (*antaryāmin*) form which is seen in the different manifestations (*avatāra*) of Bhagavān. The impersonal form or Brahman can be known by the path of knowledge. Vallabha subordinates this to the highest personal form, thereby reversing the priority of Śaṃkara, who considered the impersonal or quality-less Brah-

11. Cf. G. N. Joshi, *Atman and Moksa* (Ahmedabad : Gujarat University, 1965), p. 592.

man the highest goal and object of knowledge. Instead Vallabha in his consideration of the *Bhāgavata* brings together all the passages which highlight the supremacy of devotion and its goal the personal Bhagavān. For Vallabha, Bhagavān's creative energy obscures his bliss dimension. Devotion alone penetrates the veil of the creative energy to the bliss of Bhagavān. Bondage is considered in order to know what liberation is. Kṛṣṇa is the purport (*tātparya*) of every text. The *Vedas* had described the form of Bhagavān which was devoid of qualities, now their insufficient view of Bhagavān is supplemented and completed by the *Bhāgavata*, which describes Bhagavān as the fullness of qualities.

The key text in the *Bhāgavata* for Vallabha is I.3.28: "Kṛṣṇa indeed is Bhagavān himself."[12] This statement is given its full value and no other text can contradict its meaning. One who worships Kṛṣṇa with devotion is relieved of all misery. His motive in all things is sport (*līlā*), the motive of Bhagavān. Knowledge without devotion is useless since devotion supplies what is lacking in the path of knowledge, namely, a keen sense of Kṛṣṇa's personality. The fruit or reward of knowledge is inadequate. Since the individual self is a part (*aṃśa*) of Bhagavān, his grace alone is a sufficient instrument for bringing about the highest attainment of Bhagavān. Knowledge leads to the impersonal (*akṣara*) Brahman, but devotion leads to the bliss of Bhagavān Kṛṣṇa.

The theme of canto ten is, according to Vallabha, *nirodha*, which he defines as "a favorable condition for the divine sport along with his powers."[13] Kṛṣṇa's manifestation takes place on behalf of his devotees, whom Bhagavān wants to infuse with his bliss aspect. Vallabha says that "blazing fire, when stationed outside cannot enter a piece of wood and light the fire existing (potentially) in the wood, and that the fire existing (potentially) in the wood cannot burn the wood by itself."[14] The special intervention of Bhagavān Kṛṣṇa in his fullness is needed to bring the bliss which is already potentially in the devotee to

12. I.3.28a :... kṛṣṇastu bhagavānsvayam/
13. *Subodhinī* X.1.1, quoted in Marfatia, *The Philosophy of Vallabhācārya*, p. 219.
14. *Ibid.*, p. 221.

manifestation. Although Kṛṣṇa pervades the individual selves, his bliss is obscured and is only potential in them. If Kṛṣṇa does not reveal his manifest form, the bliss in the individual remains obscured. Thus Kṛṣṇa undertakes his play (*līlā*) in the world in order to reveal the bliss already present, but obscured, in the individual selves and in inanimate beings.

Vallabha in his commentary of X.1.12 gives an etymology of the name 'Kṛṣṇa', which is divided into *kṛṣ*, existence, and *ṇa*, bliss. Kṛṣṇa is the union of existence and bliss. Listening to his exploits realizes in the devotee his obscured existence and bliss. The devotee must abandon everything that impedes devotion, yet alone he can do nothing. By the grace of Bhagavān, every obstacle can be overcome. *Prasāda*, favor, is the manifestation of the glory of Bhagavān, while *anugraha*, grace, is the overlooking by Bhagavān of the weaknesses of the devotee. Bhagavān is the husband of the individual self which is considered feminine. God is the highest form of bliss (*rāsa*). Devotion is a constant, "firm and supreme love for God preceded by a full comprehension of his greatness."[15] Union is not the final end here, because it is already present metaphysically. When the bliss of union, as in the ecstatic play of Kṛṣṇa with the cowherd girls, occurs, it is only a transitory feeling of emotion (*vyabhicāri*), which deepens and enhances the true end of devotion which is devotion itself. There is no room here for any earthly passion (*kāma*). The ecstatic play (*rāsalīlā*) is an allegory of the love of God for his devotees in terms of the human passions of union and separation. Separation is the highest form of devotion since in it the heart hungers and craves for Kṛṣṇa, whom it perceives in everything. The ecstatic play of the cowherd girls symbolizes the ideal of unselfish devotion and total dedication to Kṛṣṇa. Their love is a spiritual love for Kṛṣṇa, untainted by physical desire. It is the ideal towards which the devotee should strive.

Vallabha systematizes the *Bhāgavata*'s statements and divides the individual selves into three kinds. These souls differ accord-

15. *Tattvārtha Dīpa Nibandha* I.42 : māhātmyajñānapūrvastu sudṛḍhaḥ sarvato'dhikaḥ/ sneho bhaktiriti proktastayā muktirna cānyathā// Quoted in Marfatia, *The Philosophy of Vallabhācārya*, p. 84.

ing to their innate essence (*svabhāva*), their behavior (*kriyā*), and the reward (*phala*) awaiting them. (1) the continuing (*pravāhika*) souls have their material cause in God's intellect, which desires to be many. There is no special providence watching over them. Since they indulge in sensuous worldly enjoyment, they are forsaken by divine grace and are not subject to divine law. They will wander in the cycle of death and rebirth forever since God does not pervade them in any special way, beyond that of his creative energy which supports their existence. Thus they have *māyā* bodies. An example of the continuing souls in the *Bhāgavata* is an *asura* (demon).

(2) Law-abiding (*maryāda*) souls are based on the divine word (*vāc*) for their material cause. They follow the divine law and study the *Vedas*. The knowledge aspect of Bhagavān predominates in them. If they seek the rewards of their actions (*sakāma*), they will be exalted in this world and in a future paradise. If they forsake the reward of their actions (*niṣkāma*), seek detachment and follow a path of knowledge or Yoga, they will have an appropriate reward. They may worship the Lord for the sake of liberation, in which case they will be absorbed in the impersonal Brahman without qualities as is appropriate for their nature.

(3) Grace (*puṣṭi*) souls evolve from the bliss (*ānanda*) aspect of the manifestation body of Bhagavān. They are the souls chosen by the Lord for participation in his exalted qualities. Within them is a seed of the divine love, which makes them fit to touch, see, and embrace Kṛṣṇa. They rely on the grace and love of God. These souls act only out of love for Bhagavān for his own sake. Led on by Bhagavān, they appropriate the divine bliss in place of their own limited essence, which had obscured that bliss. Reintegration into that bliss is the meaning of their liberation and beatitude. There are four gradations of grace souls. (a) Continuing grace (*pravāha puṣṭi*) souls are content to perform the duties of their caste and state in life. They lack the devotional fervor or affection for the Lord of higher souls, yet they are eligible by the grace of Bhagavān for a higher state in a future life. (b) Law-abiding grace (*maryāda puṣṭi*) souls know the attributes of the Lord. (c) Pure grace (*śuddha puṣṭi*) souls overflow with love for Bhagavān Kṛṣṇa. They are untainted

by his creative energy and no attribute of the divine splendor is suppressed in them. They dwell with Kṛṣṇa in Goloka, the heavenly Vṛndāvana. Their purpose in becoming manifest is to do Bhagavān's will.

According to Vallabha the exploits of Kṛṣṇa in Vṛndāvana are entirely symbolic. The birth of Kṛṣṇa is a revelation of the glorious divine form within the mind of the devotee. The death of the demoness Pūtanā is the eradication of that ignorance which binds the devotee to the world of matter. When Yaśodā sees the entire universe within Kṛṣṇa's mouth, it is a symbol of the awakening of the devotee to his true nature. The development of the intensity of devotion reveals in turn the Brahman, the Highest Self, and the Bhagavān forms of the Deity. The devotee, before entering the transcendental realm of Vṛndāvana, must put off both his physical and subtle bodies as the *Bhāgavata* says: "When the cowherd girls came together with him, they recognized the Highest Self as a paramour, their bonds disappeared and at that moment their bodies consisting of the qualities were cast off."[16] Therefore Vallabha states that there was no sexual intemperance in the ecstatic play since the cowherd girls had an essence of perfectly pure goodness (*viśuddhasattva*). As S. Bhaṭṭācārya says, "*rāsa* is to be understood as a feature of the eternal Kṛṣṇa and of the historical Kṛṣṇa at all."[17]

Vallabha thus teaches a form of predestination which seems foreign to the simplicity of the *Bhāgavata*'s teaching. He wants to protect the divine majesty, which cannot be restricted since Bhagavān's will is unconditioned. Bhagavān saves or condemns whenever he wills. In other words, he allows the level of phenomenal experience according to the whims of his play (*līlā*). In any case, he is the only existent. Ultimately there is no other, although this does not preclude the eternal existence of his parts, the individual selves. Vallabha emphasizes the *Bhāgavata*'s love devotion (*premabhakti*) in a spiritualized form. Its goal is an everlasting ecstatic dance with Kṛṣṇa in a transcendental Vṛndāvana. This sacrifices some of the historical realism of the *Bhāgavata*'s

16. X.29.11 : tameva paramātmānaṃ jārabuddhyāpi saṃgatāḥ/ jahurguṇamayaṃ dehaṃ sadyaḥprakṣīṇabandhanāḥ//

17. Bhaṭṭācārya, *The Philosophy of the Śrīmad-Bhāgavata*, I. 103.

account of the manifestation (*avatāra*) of Kṛṣṇa. Vallabha strengthens the type of devotion practiced by the cowherd girls of Vraja by means of his unqualified non-dualism, yet without sacrificing the separate existence of the devotee. He has ordered the *Bhāgavata* around what, according to him, is the central insight of the *Purāṇa*: Kṛṣṇa indeed is Bhagavān himself. From that starting point he takes every example of a devotee in the *Bhāgavata* and places it in an ascending hierarchy of devotion.

The School of Caitanya

Caitanya (1485-1535) was the founder of a devotional sect within Bengal Vaiṣṇavism in the early sixteenth century. Since he was primarily a saint and missionary of devotion, he left only a few devotional verses behind him. Systematization was done by his followers, especially the *gosvāmins* of Vṛndāvana, of whom Jīva is our primary source here. According to this school, God is apprehended in three ways. The follower of the path of knowledge sees God as the absolute Brahman, which has neither qualities nor sports among men. The follower of Yoga understands by God the Highest Self, who is the creator, maintainer, and destroyer of the universe and the inner controller of the individual self. He is the immanent aspect of Bhagavān. Then there is the follower of the path of devotion. Bhagavān is the highest personal form of the Absolute, who displays himself to the devotee in all his qualities, powers, and sports. He is both transcendent and immanent. Bhagavān Kṛṣṇa is Brahman, the Highest Self, and Bhagavān. Following the text, "Kṛṣṇa indeed is Bhagavān himself,"[18] the school affirms that Bhagavān is a form and aspect of Kṛṣṇa. The *Bhāgavata* which contains this key text (*mahāvākya*) is the authoritative Scripture for the followers of Caitanya. It is the summation of all the previous Scriptures. Since it was believed to have been written by Vyāsa as a commentary on the *Brahma Sūtras*, the *Bhāgavata*, and not the *Sūtras*, is commented upon by this school.

All the inhabitants of Vṛndāvana are parts of Kṛṣṇa (*svāṃśa*). They are all manifestations of the divine form. The cowherd girls,

18. I.3.28a : . . . kṛṣṇastu bhagavānsvayam/.

and especially Rādhā who is prominent in Bengal Vaiṣṇavism but not mentioned in the *Bhāgavata*, are powers (*śakti*) of Kṛṣṇa, who is the possessor of the powers (*śaktimat*). They are thus both different and non-different from Kṛṣṇa. The one single power of Kṛṣṇa is distinguished in three ways. The inner power (*antaraṅgā*) displays the heavenly world and all that is in it before the inner eye of Bhagavān. In this world Kṛṣṇa sports with his companions. This power is all-perfect, consisting of the divine essence of being, knowledge, and bliss (*saccidānanda*). As the Highest Self (*paramātman*), Kṛṣṇa has two other powers. The outer power (*bahiraṅgā*) is that power by which God creates, maintains, and destroys the universe. Between the inner and outer powers of Bhagavān is the expressive power (*taṭasthā*) which expresses itself in the individual selves.

Kṛṣṇa is Bhagavān, not an *avatāra*. His descent at the end of the Dvāpara age, described in the *Bhāgavata*, is not properly a manifestation. The earthly Vṛndāvana, Mathurā, and Dvāraka are identical with their heavenly counterparts. At times the sports af Kṛṣṇa, which go on eternally in the heavenly cities, are not manifest in the earthly cities. What appears to be a descent of Kṛṣṇa is only a temporary manifestation for the sake of the devotees of what is really eternal in heaven.

Kṛṣṇa, although content within his interior life, also is a self-differentiating God, who creates and enters into the universe. In the form of the presiding manifestations (*vyūha*) Kṛṣṇa evolves the universe. In the form of the cosmic manifestations (*guṇāvatāra*), Viṣṇu, Brahmā, and Śiva, then in the form of the play manifestations (*līlāvatāra*), Rāma, the tortoise, etc., and then in the form of the part manifestations (*āveśāvatāra*), Vyāsa, Nārada, etc., Kṛṣṇa watches over and compenetrates every phase of the universe and of the individual selves. Distinct from these manifestations, which are forms of Kṛṣṇa, are the individual selves (*jīva*). Yet, although distinct from Kṛṣṇa, the individual selves participate in his essence in an infinitesimal form whereas Kṛṣṇa possesses his essence perfectly and infinitely. What a drop of water is to the ocean, the individual self is to Kṛṣṇa. The self is a spark of the fire of the divine essence. It is eternal, that is, although subject to the evolution of the world from the primal nature, it stands by itself in undivided time. Its connection with the material body is unessential.

The Bengal school carries the personalization of Brahman to its furthermost. While the outer power (*bahiraṅgā*) exercised in the world of the primal nature does not affect Kṛṣṇa's essence, the inner power (*antaraṅgā*) is paradigmatic and transcendentally parallel to the outer power. Kṛṣṇa is transcendentally a man (*narākṛti*) in his interior essence. As P. Johanns puts it:

> The devotees shed tears of tenderness when they meditate on this their God adjusting His innermost life to the heart of man. They consider it as the apex of condescension, that even life as a Bhagavān or Paramātman has no meaning for Him unless it expresses itself and culminates in a likeness to human ways. It is as if God said: my life is nothing to me, except insofar as it has a meaning for souls.[19]

The Caitanya school teaches a radical metaphysical anthropomorphism. The phenomenal world and the individual self are just shadows of the transcendental world and the Supreme Self.

In this system the paths of action, knowledge, and Yoga have value only if they prepare the way for devotion. Devotion is an all-absorbing passion (*anurāga*) for God, but it also has its stages. First is devotion which resorts to means (*sādhana bhakti*) and is twofold. Prescribed devotion (*vaidhī bhakti*) follows the instructions of the *Bhāgavata* for the practice of the ninefold devotion, hearing, singing, remembering about Bhagavān, etc. A second form of the devotion which resorts to means is the devotion of emotional attachment (*rāgānuga bhakti*) to Kṛṣṇa, which bypasses the steps of prescribed devotion. It takes the form of vicarious identification of the devotee with the servants, friends, parents, and lovers of Kṛṣṇa. The goal of the devotion which resorts to means is affective devotion (*bhāva bhakti*) which is the emotional dawn of love (*preman*) for Kṛṣṇa. Love is spontaneous and exclusive attachment to Kṛṣṇa.

19. Pierre Johanns, S. J., *A Synopsis of To Christ Through the Vedanta* (Ranchi : Catholic Press, 1944). IV, 12.

At this point Bengal Vaiṣṇavism incorporates the theory of the sentiments (*rasa*) from Sanskrit aesthetics. The sentiment, or aesthetic stirring, enables the devotee to contemplate the inner life of Bhagavān Kṛṣṇa. Just as in a drama where the spectator experiences the joys and sorrows of the hero, the devotee contemplates the transcendental life of Kṛṣṇa described in the *Bhāgavata*. He relives Kṛṣṇa's life and realizes it within himself in terms of the sentiments. The highest, most perfect sentiment is the erotic thrill (*sṛṅgāra*), the highest accomplishment of devotion. For example, the cowherd girls surrendered unconditionally to Kṛṣṇa, whom they loved for his own sake. They seek nothing but to foster his pleasure. They forget their parents, husbands, and good reputation and blindly follow Kṛṣṇa. Yet there is no touch of scandal, for as Jīva Gosvāmin postulates, there are two aspects to the ecstatic play of Kṛṣṇa. As unmanifest (*aprakṛta*) in the inner essence of Kṛṣṇa, the ecstatic play takes place in a transcendental, ideally pure realm. The cowherd girls are Kṛṣṇa's intrinsic powers (*svarūpaśakti*), and thus are his wives untouched by immorality. As manifest (*prakṛta*) in the outer essence of Kṛṣṇa, the ecstatic play is a projection of the unmanifest ecstatic play. As such it is not subject to criticism. The manifest play leads the devotee by means of ecstatic devotion to the unmanifest play. The Vṛndāvana play is not a mere allegory or symbol but literally history in both its phases. But why then are the cowherd girls described in the *Bhāgavata* as the wives of other men ?

Jīva draws on the *Bharata Nāṭyaśāstra* for his explanation: "The intensity of love reaches its climax when it is impeded by constant obstacles and the meeting of the lovers takes place in concealment and that also very rarely."[20] The pitch of emotional attachment, according to traditional Sanskrit drama, reaches a greater height in the irregular love of the unmarried than in the normal love of the married. This is the way one should love Kṛṣṇa. The *Bhāgavata* describes the cowherd girls as the wives of others in the manifest play, although in the unmanifest play they are Kṛṣṇa's wives, because in the ecstatic devotion

20. Quoted in Bhaṭṭācārya, *The Philosophy of the Śrīmad-Bhāgavata*, I, 104.

(*rāsa bhakti*) of the devotee a greater attachment to Kṛṣṇa can be thus reached. In this way Jīva transformed the *Bhāgavata*'s preference for the devotion of separation (*viraha bhakti*) into one free from scandal by drawing on the Sanskrit theory of the drama.

The Caitanya school describes its teaching as ineffable difference-in-identity (*acintyabhedābheda*). Metaphysically Bhagavān realizes himself in the world, although he is already perfectly realized in his interior essence. He is the cause of all, and in his causal state already contains every effect, yet proceeds for the sake of the devotee, who is already transcendentally present in Bhagavān, to externalize himself. Mystically the devotee realizes himself in Bhagavān, although he is already Bhagavān in his expressive power (*taṭasthā*). This identity is metaphysically and mystically ineffable (*acintya*). In a mysterious manner Bhagavān's powers are different from his essence, yet one with him. The primary analogue for this mystery is the relation of lovers, which is a difference-in-identity relationship, whose rapture reenforces both difference and identity. This difference-in-identity is found both in Kṛṣṇa's love for his devotee, which finds expression both metaphysically and cosmically, and in the devotee's love for Kṛṣṇa, where its mystical (*rasa*) expression completes the purpose of Kṛṣṇa's play.

The Caitanya school is based primarily on the *Bhāgavata*, interpreted according to the kind of erotic mysticism experienced by Caitanya and his followers. This mysticism seeks to express its religious longings in terms of the *Bhāgavata*, especially its tenth canto. It seeks to relive that story. The Vṛndāvana exploits of Kṛṣṇa overshadow completely the parts of his biography which took place in Mathurā and Dvāraka. The mutual love of the devotee and Bhagavān is emphasized much more than in the original *Purāṇa*. The figure of Rādhā, who is barely hinted at in the *Bhāgavata*, is given prominence. Thus the *Bhāgavata* whose stories were developed, for instance in the *Padma Purāṇa*[21] and in the *Brahmavaivarta Purāṇa*, is interpreted in the light of those developments.

21. Cf. Sushil Kumar De, *Early History of the Vaishnava Faith and Movement in Bengal* (Calcutta : Firma K. L. Mukhopadhyay, 1961), p. 347.

Summary

In the interpretations of these schools various facets of the *Bhāgavata* are emphasized. As with any authoritative, canonical Scripture, the *Bhāgavata* reenforced and gave form to the religious experiences of its followers. In turn it was seen and read through the eyes of those experiences, and thus received a form and sense over and beyond the literal sense. None of the schools gives a redaction criticism of the *Bhāgavata*. They were not in a position to, if they had wanted. Religiously all the interpretations are valid within the parameters of their hermeneutical principles. Madhva, in order to emphasize the supremacy of Bhagavān, interpreted the non-duality or identity passages in a metaphorical sense. Madhva was devoted to Viṣṇu, thus he backtracked somewhat from the *Bhāgavata*'s identification of the Supreme Deity with Kṛṣṇa. The fact that he was at pains to interpret the non-duality passages in this way is a good clue that the redactor intended them to be understood in a normal Vedāntic and non-dual manner. Since the ecstatic play of Kṛṣṇa with the cowherd girls was contrary to his understanding of devotion, it was downplayed.

Vallabha stressed the non-dualist quality of the *Bhāgavata*. He wrote a commentary on the *Brahma Sūtras* in the light of the *Bhāgavata*. This anachronism irks modern scholars but is perfectly consistent with his religious motivation. He identified the Supreme Deity with Kṛṣṇa. Because of his strong aversion for the illusion (*māyā*) doctrine of Śaṃkara and his followers, he stressed the non-illusion aspects of the *Bhāgavata*'s teaching on the creative energy (*māyā*) of Bhagavān. In this matter he approximated the intention of the redactor. His concern to accommodate the *Bhāgavata* to the Vedānta traditions gives his interpretation a Vedānta flavor. This too is in accord with the redactor's intent. Finally he systematized, in the doctrine of the different levels of devotion, what was an eclectic collection of the legends of famous devotees.

The followers of Caitanya were even more single-minded about the *Bhāgavata* than Madhva or Vallabha. The emotional intensity of Caitanya's devotion to Kṛṣṇa and the Vṛndāvana play was an ever-present example of what they thought was the *Bhāgavata*'s teaching. Devotion in this school became a vicarious participation in the Kṛṣṇa *līlā*. Following the lead of the *Bhāgavata*, the stories of the great devotees become histories, which are more real than the very life experiences of the devotee. As he advances in devotion, the devotee ceases to live in an earthly Vṛndāvana but in a transcendental realm inhabited by Kṛṣṇa frolicking with the cowherd girls.

The *Bhāgavata* teaches non-dualism. It also teaches the distinction between Bhagavān and the individual self. Depending upon the predilection of the interpreter a system of non-dualism, dualism, or difference-in-identity results. These interpretations shed light on the redactor's intent. It becomes clear, however, that a major influence on all of the interpreters, but not upon the redactor, was the illusion (*māyā*) doctrine of Śaṃkara. The *Bhāgavata* also teaches two forms of devotion. Depending upon the predilection of the interpreter, a meditative devotion or an emotional devotion results. These interpretations, whether inclusive or one-sided, place the unsystematic quality of the *Bhāgavata*'s teaching about devotion in high relief.

CHAPTER VIII

THE RELIGIOUS STRUCTURE OF THE *BHĀGAVATA*

Non-dualism and Difference-in-Identity

The *Bhāgavata*, according to its own account, is a treatise on the meaning of Brahman (*āśraya*), which is the support and refuge of the devotees. All its other topics and characteristics are devoted to explaining the ramifications of Brahman. Brahman is above all the Supreme Deity, Bhagavān Kṛṣṇa. Yet in the very first verse of the *Bhāgavata*, Brahman, the highest reality, is connected with the universe: "Him from whom is the creation, etc. of the universe."[1] In the first canto Sūta declares the non-dual nature of this absolute reality: "Those who possess the knowledge of the Truth call the knowledge of non-duality as the Truth; it is called Brahman, the Highest Self and Bhagavān."[2] The *Bhāgavata* thus clearly appeals to the non-dualist tradition of Vedānta as the framework for its assertions about the non-dual nature of the Absolute, who is identified with Bhagavān Kṛṣṇa.

There is a Vedāntic core which is common to all the schools and Scriptures of Vedānta. It may be summarized in this way. Brahman is the supreme cause of the universe and is all-pervading and eternal. This is known from Scripture: the *Upaniṣads*, the *Brahma Sūtras*, and the *Bhagavad Gītā*. Actions are subordinate to knowledge or devotion. They are useful only for preparing the mind for knowledge or devotion. This accom-

1. I.1.1a : janmādyasya yato.../
2. I.2.11 : vadanti tattattvavidastattvaṃ yajjñānamadvayam/ brahmeti paramātmeti bhagavāniti śabdyate//

plished, the actions and their rewards must be renounced. Bondage is subjection to the cycle of death and rebirth (*saṃsāra*). Liberation is a deliverance from that cycle.

In the Vaiṣṇava tradition the doctrine of devotion is added to this Vedāntic core. Devotion is then the means of achieving liberation. Brahman is seen as a personal God who has an infinite number of attributes or qualities. The individual selves retain some degree of individuality even in liberation. The selves are atomic and share Brahman's attributes of knowing and acting. Liberation becomes a greater participation in the nature of Bhagavān.[3]

Non-dualism is a profound insight into the nature of Brahman. Vaiṣṇavism transformed non-dualism by means of its intense theism, which necessitated some means of acknowledging the reality of the world and of the individual self. One such means within the ambit of non-dualism is the doctrine of difference-in-identity (*bhedābheda*). No specific school is referred to here by that doctrine. Rather it is a classification of a generic, although variously nuanced, position within the spectrum of the Hindu thought tradition. There may be some confusion in regard to the relation of the difference-in-identity theory to non-dualism. Non-dualism is that position which bases itself upon the *Upaniṣads*. It speculates about the non-duality, or identity, of Brahman, the Highest Self, and the individual self. As such it stands in need of further explanation as to how that can be. The manner of explaining the non-duality is the basis for differentiating types of non-dualism. Generally two types of non-dualism have been distinguished within Hinduism.

That position which denies the ultimate reality of the world and of the individual self while positing a single absolute reality, Brahman, whose nature is pure consciousness, may be called a non-dualism which is without distinctions (*nirviśeṣādvaita*). Brahman is described as without qualities (*nirguṇa*) or as without distinctions or differences (*abheda*). The concepts of illusion (*māyā*) and ignorance (*avidyā*) are introduced to give some

3. V. S. Ghate, *The Vedānta : A Study of the Brahma Sūtras with Bhāṣyas of Śaṃkara, Rāmānuja, Nimbārka, Madhva, and Vallabha* (Poona : Bhandarkar Oriental Research Institute, 1960), pp. 36-37.

explanation for the unreality of the phenomenal world. This view of non-dualism is held by Śaṃkara and the *māyāvādins*.

That position which affirms that the reality of the world and of the individual self is ontologically dependent upon a single absolute reality, Brahman, whose nature may be qualified or particularized, may be called a non-dualism which has qualities or distinctions (*saviśeṣādvaita*). Another term for this is difference-in-identity (*bhedābheda*). Brahman is described as with qualities (*saguṇa*) or with distinctions or differences (*sabheda*). The concepts of creative energy (*māyā*) and of power (*śakti*) are introduced to give some explanation for the dependent reality of the phenomenal world. This is probably the position of the *Brahma Sūtras*. With various nuances this position is held by Bhāskara, Vijñānabhikṣu, and by the Vaiṣṇava theologians, Nimbārka, Rāmānuja, Vallabha, and the followers of Caitanya.[4]

There are five characteristics of Vaiṣṇava difference-in-identity theology.[5] (1) The world which is real has its origin in Brahman or God, who is both its efficient and material cause. (2) The individual self, although distinct, is ultimately identified with God. (3) Bondage is in some sense the responsibility of the individual self; liberation is freely given by God. (4) God, the ultimate reality, is personal. (5) The Divine penetrates all strata of reality, since there is no other reality.

A further position may be identified in Hindu thought. Dualism (*dvaita*) is that position which affirms that the relation between Brahman or God and the world and the individual self is one of ultimate difference. This difference or distinction is fundamental. God is the efficient but not the material cause of the universe and the individual self. This position is espoused by Madhva and his followers.

4. *Ibid.*, p. 170.

5. Cf. John W. Borelli, Jr., "The Theology of Vijñānabhikṣu : A Translation of His Commentary on *Brahma Sūtras* I.1.2 and an Exposition of His Difference-in-Identity Theology," unpublished Ph.D. dissertation, Fordham University, 1976, although Vijñānabhikṣu's difference-in-identity theology differs significantly from that of the Vaiṣṇava theologians.

The following chart illustrates these distinctions :

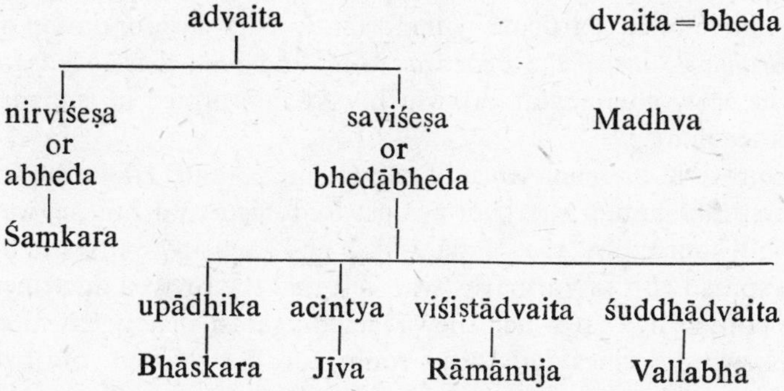

As we can see, difference-in-identity (*bhedābheda*) is open to several interpretations. Thus from the point of view of the identity of Brahman, Vedāntic theology may be classified into two positions : non-dualism (*advaita*), divided between (1) non-dualism without differences (*abheda*) and difference-in-identity (bhedābheda), and (2) dualism (*dvaita*), while from the point of view of difference between God and the world it may be classified into three positions : (1) non-dualism without qualities (*abheda*), (2) difference-in-identity (*bhedābheda*), and (3) dualism (*bheda*).

In its implicit religious structure the *Bhāgavata* is a difference-in-identity text. Explicitly it is non-dualist. At the time in the ninth century in the milieu of South India, non-dualism was virtually equivalent to difference-in-identity. A text was non-dualist which upheld the non-dual reality of the Absolute with qualities since the new form of non-dualism without qualities stemming from Śaṃkara was only beginning to make its influence felt. Several centuries later by the time of the systematic theologians (*ācārya*) that influence was formidable and had to be reckoned with. For instance, according to the best scholarship, the *Brahma Sūtras*, even though its doctrine is explicable only in the most general terms, taught a non-dualism of the difference-in-identity variety. The illusion (*māyā*) doctrine of Śaṃkara finds no support in a literal reading of the *Brahma Sūtras*. The same is true of the *Purāṇas* and the Pāñcarātra literature. So powerful, however, was the illusion doctrine's influence and so cogent was its claim to be understood as non-dualism, that once it was known, scholastic Vedāntins had to take notice of it. Particularly important was its appropriation of the *Brahma Sūtras*, the *Bhagavad Gītā*, and even the *Bhāgavata* (by its early commentators), which were interpreted in support of its teaching.

The revival or renaissance of Brahmanism and Hinduism in the first millennium A.D. over against Buddhism and Jainism was strongly spurred by the Mīmāṃsākas and then by Śaṃkara. It soon spread to the Vaiṣṇavas who felt that the revived doctrines were tainted by that which they reacted against. They felt that these new doctrines left little room for the religion of love and devotion, which had a long tradition among them. As R. G. Bhandarkar remarks : "This doctrine left no room for the exercise of love and piety in the world of reality, though its followers allow it in the ordinary illusive condition of the human souls, and therefore it laid the axe at the root of Vaiṣṇavism."[6] The result was the attempt by the scholastic Vaiṣṇava theologians to recapture their own documents, which they considered their heritage. Their counterattacks employed more finely honed interpretative principles than before. The postulation of non-dualism was not enough, since the *māyāvādins* also claimed to have reached the true meaning of non-dualism and the true interpretation of the Scriptures. Therefore the Śrī-Vaiṣṇavas brought forth qualified non-dualism, Nimbārka taught a dualistic non-dualism (*dvaitādvaita*), and others attempted variations on the non-dualism with qualities theme. Madhva tried a new tack altogether and advocated dualism (*dvaita*). These scholastic theologians were more or less successful in combatting the illusion theory and in giving ontological support to the relation of the devotee to Bhagavān in devotion. We have seen in Chapter VII the various hermeneutical uses to which they applied the *Bhāgavata Purāṇa*.

The Bhāgavata's Difference-in-Identity

That the Bhāgavata is explicitly non-dualist and implicitly difference-in-identity can easily be shown by appeal to its many

6. R. G. Bhandarkar, *Vaiṣṇavism, Śaivism and Minor Religious Systems* (Varanasi : Indological Book House, 1965), p. 51.

theistic passages which propose non-dualism in contexts which support the reality of the world and of the individual self. In canto two the *Bhāgavata* presumes a difference-in-identity structure: "Bhagavān assumes the form of Brahmā and accepts names, forms, and activities, himself being both the things designated and the words denoting them. He is both the doer of actions, and non-doer. He is beyond both."[7] Passages like this one are fresh and naive, uncomplicated by a theory of transcendental illusion. Again in canto three, Viṣṇu tells Brahmā that "when you are full of devotion and properly poised in meditation, you will see me pervading you and the world, and yourself and the world reposing in me."[8] The Absolute is all that is and he contains all subordinate reality. Difference-in-identity theory grounds the evolution and dissolution of the universe by means of Bhagavān's creative energy : "By the power of the creative energy of myself, in association with the elements, senses, and the qualities, I create myself in my self, protect them and destroy them; the Self is an embodiment of knowledge, pure, separate, unconnected with the qualities."[9] Difference-in-identity is the implicit structure which allows the Absolute to be one and many at the same time.

That a difference-in-identity form of non-dualism is implicit in the *Bhāgavata* is corroborated by its Sāṃkhya passages. The ultimate reality is one and beginningless. Superior to primal nature (*prakṛti*), the Absolute shines forth in all the evolutes and all the individual selves. In order to realize himself for some ineffable purposes of his own, he disturbed the equilibrium of the latent constituent qualities of his power. This is done through the instrumentality of time. The result is primal nature, which then proceeded to evolve all the other categories. Yet these were still in a latent state. They became manifest through the creative energy of the Person (*puruṣa*) form of Bhagavān. The absolute

7. II.10.36 : sa vācyavācakatayā bhagavān brahmarūpadhṛk/ nāmarūpakriyā dhatte sakarmā' karmakaḥ paraḥ//

8. III.9.31 : tata ātmani loke ca bhaktiyuktaḥ samāhitaḥ/ draṣṭā'si māṃ tataṃ brahman mayi lokāṃstvamātmanaḥ//

9. X.47.30-31a : ātmanyevātmanātmānaṃ sṛje hanmyanupālaye/ ātmamāyānubhāvena bhūtendriyaguṇātmanā// ātmā jñānamayaḥ śuddho vyatirikto' guṇānvayaḥ/

transcendent Deity willingly foregoes his transcendent state for immersion in lesser states of reality. The result is the manifest universe and the individual selves pervaded by Bhagavān in three forms : as their material cause, their efficient cause, and their inner controller. Bhagavān is also the final cause since all things will return to latency within the divine essence. The individual self loses sight of its origin and goal through ignorance, which is caused by the creative energy, and thinks itself a reality independent of the chain of being. The Supreme Self by its own creative energy has made itself subject to its own power in a difference-in-identity relationship. The Sāṃkhya of the *Bhāgavata* while establishing the separateness of the evolutes also emphasizes the non-difference quality of all things within the absolute Supreme Being.

The definitive identification of Bhagavān with Kṛṣṇa gives the Deity a radically anthropomorphic form. The difference-in-identity relationship is emphasized by the metaphor of the human person. The Cosmic Person, originally conceived of as Viṣṇu or Nārāyaṇa, but now as Kṛṣṇa, encompasses all beings in an organic unity. The universe is the embodiment of Bhagavān and the individual selves coalesce within the Highest Self. When this Cosmic Person is joined to the personal biography of Kṛṣṇa, the prince and the cowherd, a potent religious dynamism transforms the traditional meditative forms of devotion. The force of contemplative union or non-difference is held in tension with a lover's feeling of separation. The primary analogue for the relation of the individual self to the Highest Self is transferred from knowledge to the level of feeling. Drama replaces psychology. The non-dual Brahman's creation of others finds a motive. Whereas knowledge discovers that Brahman is being (*sat*), this intensive devotion uncovers a blissful Bhagavān, eager to share, to experience the fullness of his rapture with another. The experience of the rapture of the devotee for Bhagavān is Bhagavān delighting in himself. Devotion is the condescension of the bliss of Bhagavān toward the devotee. Devotion is non-dualism and difference-in-identity rapturously experienced. In the *Bhāgavata* if there is to be a real bond between the devotee and Bhagavan, it must be intrinsic to Bhagavān as well as to the devotee. "God stoops to the mind of men," according to S. Bhaṭṭācārya, "to establish the triumph of basic unity between man and Himself."[10] Devotion is Bhagavān. The flow of the mind toward Bhagavān, vitiated by no personal motive, triumphs even over liberation. All sense of a selfish 'I' and 'mine' is lost in the bliss of love, but the basis for a personal relationship with Bhagavān is granted by his grace. Devotion itself becomes the only distinguishing characteristic between the devotee and Bhagavān.

Nowhere is this difference-in-identity better expressed in the *Bhāgavata* than in the ecstatic dance of Kṛṣṇa with the cowherd girls. The cowherd girls have stripped away every trace of 'I' and 'mine' in their selfless loving regard for Kṛṣṇa. He rewards each of them with the highest bliss of his own personal presence. The dance has no beginning and no end. The *Bhāgavata* stretches every metaphor, simile and analogy of the Purāṇic tradition to their limit in order to express the splendor of devotion to Bhagavān Kṛṣṇa who unites himself to the devotee. Devotion for Bhagavān finds a metaphysical basis in a difference-in-identity form of non-dualism which in turn is grounded on the experience of devotion.

10. Bhaṭṭācārya, *The Philosophy of the Śrīmad-Bhāgavata*, II, 156.

CHAPTER IX

CONCLUSION

This study of the religious structure of the *Bhāgavata Purāṇa*, although technical and analytical, has a significance and meaning for the life and study of religion beyond that of situating a Scriptural text within a religious history. Reflection on some of its basic elements shows that this text engages the basic issues confronting a person seeking to reach and authentic existence. In it deep and unconscious forces working in the religious life of humans have come into the area of explicit consciousness. The *Bhāgavata* is above all God-conscious. In it God is continually breaking into the world of man. He gives solace, fights off demons, counsels, plays, sports, and confers wisdom. The *Purāṇa* is what happens when religious men seek to put together in one text every aspect, implication, and significance of that breaking into the human realm. *The Purāṇa of the Devotees of Bhagavān* is what happens when those devotees compile and collate every bit of data about their beloved Kṛṣṇa, every saying, sermon, anecdote, legend, story, incident, or teaching which will explain his coming among men. Like the Bible, this *Purāṇa* brings together creation and salvation, where we come from and where we are going. The origin and the goal of human existence implicate each other. Consistency falls before inclusivity in such a worthy task.

God is the center to which the two main themes of the *Bhāgavata* are drawn: non-dualism and devotion. Non-dualism is a radical attempt to preserve both the transcendence and the immanence of the Divine. This insight is not the result of a process of detached speculation. It is not a philosophy. Non-dualism is both a religion and a spirituality. The transcendent Deity guarantees the orderliness of the phenomenal order, the immanent

Deity glows within and bursts the bounds of that phenomenal order. God's presence overwhelms the autonomy both of the universe and of human beings. Non-dualism ties together within the unity of God all his creatures, sentient and insentient. Authentic existence is impossible, according to the *Bhāgavata*, without a vision of non-dualism. Without it all order ceases, and disorder engulfs men.

But God comes among men. Kṛṣṇa is the beloved of the devotee. He is an awesome Apollo, a god of creative order. Shining and beautiful, he shares his wisdom with his followers, taking them by the hand and showing them the path of devotion which brings salvation. Kṛṣṇa is an attractive Dionysus, a god of creative disorder. Mischievous and ecstatic, he romps with peasant women, taking their hands and dancing through the night. Kṛṣṇa is a god and a man. He brings God to men and men to God. Devotion to him is an entry into the real by means of an inner life process. It combines knowing and feeling in a path of self-transformation. Yet devotion is a grace from God. Both the state of illusion and the state of transformation are due to God's creative energy (*māyā*), which is surpassed and superseded by God's appearance among men in his truest form. The transcendent Deity, Kṛṣṇa, is like a man. Thus men are divine and God is human.

The love of the devotee for God is primary in the *Bhāgavata.* There is mention of love of neighbor only in passages about friendliness and compassion. God is all and all-encompassing. His grace and favor extend to the devotee the divine existence to be grasped in a discovery of God within the inner self. Love for and devotion to God discover the non-dualism of God and his devotee. The macrophase of God's love for men is paralleled in the microphase of men's love for God. The devotees discover that their yearning for God is an expression of God's desire to be loved. Yearning for God is a manifestation of the grace of God among men. It is God yearning for himself. The devotee is God becoming other in order to love and to be loved. God desires men to love him and thus enters the realm of human beings where he is pursued and sought for by his devotees. God descends to men so that men may ascend to God. Bhagavān is God who is sought after, the devotee is God seeking.

God is a love in which the universe and human beings participate. Because human beings are emanations of God there is a mutual participation of God in the love of men for him and of men in the love of God for them. Eros and Agape, in the sense of Anders Nygren,[1] are identical because there is no ultimate distinction between God and his devotees. To the extent that there is a distinction between God and his devotee, God represents the type of Eros-love. He spontaneously and freely loves himself and motivates his devotees to love him in order to enhance that Self-love. The universe and the devotees within it are an expression of the Self-delight of God. The devotees also participate in this Eros-love. They have an innate tendency, when it is not obstructed by ignorance and attachment to sense objects, to center their attention in a loving gaze upon a Deity who is not other than themselves. This love of the devotees is Eros because it cannot but be a fulfilment of their inner selves while at the same time it is the love of God for himself which is a fulfilment of his own Self. The ideal of Agape is represented in the *Bhāgavata* by the cowherd girls who forego all delight in the beloved Deity in a sacrifice of self. Through an act of faith in God's grace and on account of their selfless love for him their self-sacrifice becomes an expression of their absolute dependence upon and participation in the existence of God. If one can say that there is a transvaluation of Eros by Agape in Christianity, then it is true to say that in the *Bhāgavata* there is a transvaluation of Agape by Eros. The self-sacrifice of the Agape-love of the cowherd girls is drawn into the vortex of the Self-centered desire of the Eros-love of Bhagavān Kṛṣṇa.

The interaction of these two loves is grounded by the *Bhāgavata* in its difference-in-identity metaphysics. The identification of Bhagavān and his devotees makes possible their distinction. This difference-in-identity non-dualism distinguishes the devotionalism of the *Bhāgavata* from the devotionalism of the other three major devotional traditions of the world, Christianity, Islam, and Mahāyāna Buddhism. Christianity

1. Anders Nygren, *Eros and Agape*, translated by Philip S. Watson, Harper Torchbooks (New York : Harper and Row, 1969).

roots its devotion in the incarnation among men of a transcendent Deity. God is neither the 'material' cause of the universe nor of men's souls. Salvation is the mysterious bestowal of the divine life by means of grace. The primary locus of the Christian's devotion is in public liturgy in which the redemptive mystery is celebrated. While salvation is a divinization and entry into the life of the Trinity, the distinction between the devotee and Deity is always kept in view. This distinction is further emphasized and maintained in Islam. God is personal but totally other and one. Neither incarnation nor mediation can be interposed between the devotee and the one God. The paradigmatic act of devotion is an act of surrender before the majesty of God. The devotion of Mahāyāna Buddhism for the Buddha or for a Bodhisattva takes place against the background of the Non-Self or of Emptiness. In such a tradition neither identity nor difference is important. The process of salvation is primary. Whereas the other traditions view God and the devotees through the primary analogues of Being and Selfhood, Buddhism relies on the analogues of Non-Being and Non-Self. Its devotion is colored by this negative tone. The *Bhāgavata* along with most of the devotional schools of Hinduism stands over against these three devotional traditions by its emphasis on the non-duality of God and the devotee. This identity is based upon a conception of 'material' causality which is not found in the other traditions. This emphasis gives the *Bhāgavata*'s type of devotion a distinctive quality and tone quite different from that of the other traditions.

While identity is found in the other traditions, often in their esoteric or heretical phases, it is a 'moral' or 'spiritual' identity. For Christianity and Islam the accusation of pantheism limits the extent to which the language of identity can be used. Identity is thus a 'mystical' union of God and the devotee which is rendered suspect if its language of union suggests metaphysical identity. In contrast the phase of Hinduism represented by the *Bhāgavata* glories in the use of a radical language of identity. Vedāntic and Sāṃkhya thought introduces an identity based upon a 'material' causality in which the effects and their causes are identified. The identity is not to be misunderstood as implying the non-entity or illusoriness of the world. For the *Bhāgavata* non-dualism functions within a religion of devotion which maximizes the personhood of the Deity. Although each tradition of devotion characteristically maximizes the personhood of the Supreme Deity, and thus distinguishes the Deity from the person of the devotee, the *Bhāgavata* introduces this distinction within the person of the Supreme Deity. Perhaps a homologue for the nature of this distinction is the Christian doctrine of the Trinity wherein otherness does not imply separation. Rather the perfection of the Deity requires a Triune difference within the identity of the Godhead. In a homologous manner the *Bhāgavata* proposes a vision of a God who by his own power creates distinctions within himself. These distinctions derive reality from the Godhead without diminishing his reality. To separate devotion from non-dualism as has often been done is therefore to trivialize the *Bhāgavata*'s vision of the devotee's love for Kṛṣṇa. Devotion is primarily an ontological rather than a moral phenomenon.

APPENDIX I

Comparison of Bhāgavata and Classical Sāṃkhya[1]

A. *Bhāgavata Sāṃkhya*

puruṣa

Prakṛti = three guṇas = pradhāna

mahat = citta = buddhi

ahaṃkāra

sāttvika adhidaiva jñānaśakti	rājasa adhyātma kriyāśakti		tāmasa adhibhūta dravyaśakti	
manas	5 jñāna indriyas	5 karma indriyas	5 tanmātras	5 bhūtas
	śrotra	vāk	śabda	ākāśa
	tvak	pāṇi	sparśa	vāyu
	cakṣus	pāda	rūpa	tejas
	rasanā	upastha	rasa	āpas
	ghrāṇa	pāyu	gandha	pṛthvī

1. Based on the charts compiled by T. S. Rukmani, *A Critical Study of the Bhāgavata Purāṇa*, Chowkhamba Sanskrit Studies Vol. LXXVII (Varanasi : Chowkhamba Sanskrit Series Office, 1970), pp. 21 and 23. Cf. II.5.21-31; III.5.23-27; III.26.1-48; XI.24.1-9.

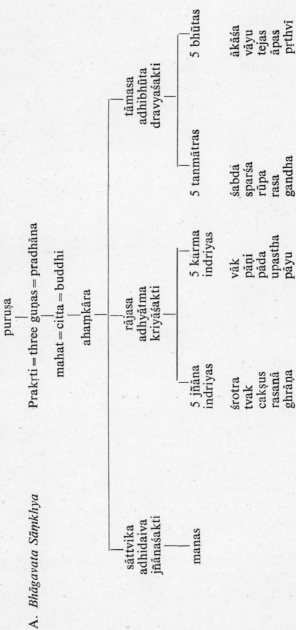

B. *Īśvarakṛṣṇa Sāṃkhya*

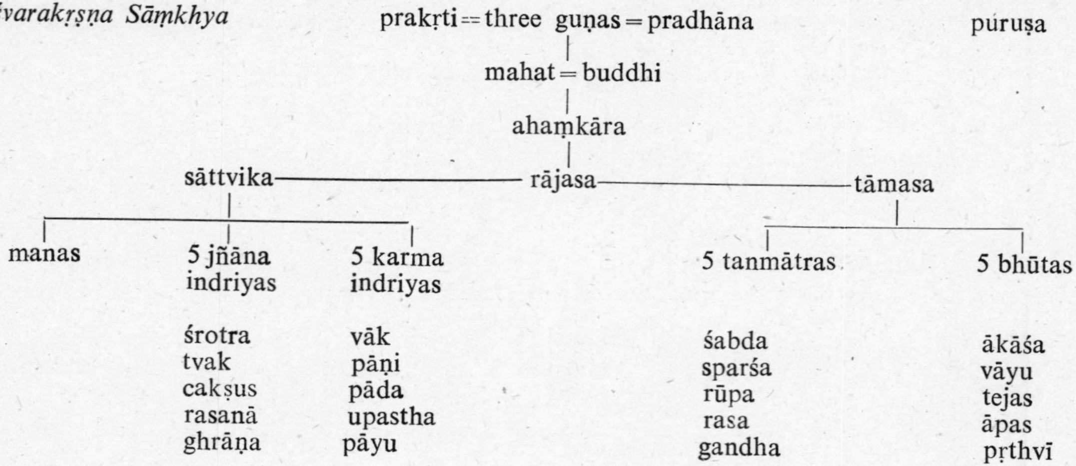
prakṛti = three guṇas = pradhāna
puruṣa
mahat = buddhi
ahaṃkāra
sāttvika
rājasa
tāmasa
manas
5 jñāna indriyas
5 karma indriyas
5 tanmātras
5 bhūtas
śrotra
tvak
cakṣus
rasanā
ghrāṇa
vāk
pāṇi
pāda
upastha
pāyu
śabda
sparśa
rūpa
rasa
gandha
ākāśa
vāyu
tejas
āpas
pṛthvī

BIBLIOGRAPHY

Texts and Translations

1. *Bhāgavata Purāṇa*

Bhāgavata Purāṇa of Kṛṣṇa Dvaipāyana Vyāsa With Sanskrit Commentary Bhāvārthabodhinī of Śrīdhara Svāmin. Edited by J. L. Shastri, Delhi : Motilal Banarsidass, 1983.

A Prose English Translation of Srimadbhagabatam. Edited and published by Manmatha Dutt. 3 vols. Calcutta : Printed by H. C. Dass, 1895-1896.

Srimad Bhagavatam. Translated by N. Raghunathan. 2 vols. Madras : Vighneswara Publishing House, 1979.

Śrīmad Bhāgavata Mahāpurāṇa (With Sanskrit text and English translation). Translated by C. L. Goswami. 2 vols. Gorakhpur : Gita Press, 1971.

Śrīmadbhāgavatamahāpurāṇam. 2 vols. Gorakhpur : Gita Press, n.d.

The Srimad-Bhagavatam of Krishna-Dwaipayana Vyasa. Translated by J. M. Sanyal. 2 vols. New Delhi : Munshiram Manoharlal Pvt. Ltd., 1973.

Śrīmad Bhāgavatam of Kṛṣṇa-Dvaipāyana Vyāsa. Translated by A. C. Bhaktivedanta. New York : Bhaktivedanta Book Trust, 1972-1982.

The Wisdom of God (Srimad Bhagavatam). Translated by Swami Prabhavananda. New York : Capricorn Books 1968. (A synopsis and paraphrase.)

2. *Other Works*

Aphorisms on the Gospel of Divine Love or Nārada Bhakti Sūtras. Translated by Swāmi Tyāgīśānanda. Mylapore, Madras : Sri Ramakrishna Math, 1972.

Sāṃkhya-Kārikā of Śrīmad Īśvarakṛṣṇa with the Māṭharavṛtti of Māṭharācārya. Edited by Sāhityācārya Pt. Viṣṇu Prasād Sarma. Varanasi: Chowkhamba Sanskrit Series Office, 1970.

A Prose English Translation of Visnupuranam. Translated by Manmatha Nath Dutt. Chowkhamba Sanskrit Studies, Vol. CX. Varanasi: Chowkhamba Sanskrit Series Office, 1972.

Śrīśrīviṣṇupurāṇa. Gorakhpur : Gita Press, n.d. (Sanskrit and Hindi texts.)

The Vedānta Sūtras of Bādarāyaṇa with the Commentary by Śaṅkara. Translated by George Thibaut. 2 parts. *Sacred Books of the East,* Vols. XXXIV and XXXVIII. Edited by Max Muller. New York : Dover Publications, Inc., 1962 [1890-1896].

Books and Articles

Anand, Subhash. "The Bhāgavata Purāṇa: A Guide for the Sādhaka."*Purāṇa,* XX (January 1978), 71-86.

———. "Bhakti—The Bhāgavata Way to God." *Purāṇa,* XXII (Jule 1980), 187-211.

———. "Saguṇa or Nirguṇa." *Purāṇa,* XXI (January, 1979), 40-63.

———. "Spiritual Discipleship as Described by the Bhagavata-Purana," *Indian Theological Studies,* XV (March 1978), 21-55.

Archer, W. G. *The Loves of Krishna in Indian Painting and Poetry.* London: George Allen & Unwin. 1957.

Banerjea, Jitendranath. *Paurāṇic and Tāntric Religion* (*Early Phase*). Calcutta : University Press, 1956.

Barz, Richard. *The Bhakti Sect of Vallabhācārya.* Faridabad: Thomson Press, 1976.

Bhaktivedanta, A. C. *Kṛṣṇa: The Supreme Personality of the Godhead.* New York: Bhaktivedanta Book Trust, 1970. 3 Vols.

Bhandarkar, R. G. *Vaiṣṇavism, Śaivism and Minor Religious Systems.* Varanasi: Indological Book House, 1965 [1913].

Bhatt, G. H. "The Place of *Bhāgavata* in the Śuddhādvaita of Vallabhācārya." *Viśveśvarānanda Indological Journal*, II (1964), 261-63.

Bhaṭṭācārya, Siddheśvara. "A Critique of the *Bhāgavata Purāṇa*." *Bihar Research Society Journal*, XXXVI (March-June, 1950), pp. 22-39.

———. *The Philosophy of the Śrīmad-Bhāgavata*. Calcutta: Ranajit Ray, 1960-1962. 2 vols.

Bhattacharji, Sukumari. *The Indian Theogony*. Cambridge : At the University Press, 1970.

Biswas, A. S. *Bhāgavata Purāṇa: A Linguistic Study*. Dibrugarh: Vishveshvaranand Book Agency, 1965.

Borelli, John W. Jr. "The Theology of Vijñānabhikṣu: A Translation of His Commentary on Brahma Sūtras I.1.2 and an Exposition of His Difference-in-Identity Theology." Unpublished Ph.D. dissertation, Fordham University, 1976.

Brown, Cheever Mackenzie, *God As Mother: A Feminine Theology in India*. Hartford, Vt.: Claude Stark, 1974.

Carman, John Braisted. *The Theology of Rāmānuja: An Essay in Inter-religious Understanding*. New Haven: Yale University Press, 1974.

Chakravarti, Sudhindra Chandra. *Philosophical Foundation of Bengal Vaiṣṇavism*. Calcutta: Academic Publishers, 1969.

Chatteyee, Chinmayi. *Studies in the Evolution of Bhakti Cult*. 2 vols. Calcutta : Jadavpur University, 1981.

Chemburkar, J. "Historical and Religious Background of the Concept of Four Yugas in the Mahābhārata and the Bhāgavata Purāṇa." *Purāṇa XVI* (January 1974), 67-76.

Dasgupta, Surendranath. *A History of Indian Philosophy*. 5 vols. Cambridge : At the University Press, 1922-1950.

De, Sushil Kumar. *Early History of the Vaisnava Faith and Movement in Bengal*. Calcutta: Firma K. L. Mukhopadhyay, 1961.

de Bary, William T., ed. *Sources of Indian Tradition*. 2 vols. New York: Columbia University Press. 1958.

Dhavamony, Mariasusai. *Love of God According to Śaiva Siddhānta : A Study in the Mysticism and Theology of Śaivism.* Oxford: At the Clarendon Press, 1971.

Dikshitar, V. R. "Kṛṣṇa in Early Tamil Literature." *Indian Culture*, IV (October 1937), 267-71.

Dowson, John. *A Classical Dictionary of Hindu Mythology and Religion, Geography, History, and Literature.* New Delhi: Oriental Books Reprint Corporation, 1973.

Gail, Adalbert. *Bhakti im Bhāgavatapurāṇa*, Wiesbaden. Otto Harrassowitz, 1969.

Ghate, V. S. *The Vedānta: A Study of the Brahma Sūtras with Bhāṣyas of Śaṃkara, Rāmānuja, Nimbārka, Madhva, and Vallabha.* Poona: Bhandarkar Oriental Research Institute, 1960.

Gonda, Jan. *Change and Continuity in Indian Religion.* Disputationes Rheno-Trajectiones, Vol. IX. The Hague: Mouton & Co., 1965.

Gonda, Jan. *Aspects of Early Viṣṇuism.* Delhi: Motilal Banarsidass, 1969 [1954].

———. *Viṣṇuism and Śivaism: A Comparison.* London: Athlone Press, 1970

Goswami, Bhagabat Kumar. *Bhakti Cult in Ancient India.* Calcutta: Banerjea, 1924.

Hacker, Paul. "Relations of Early Advaitins to Vaiṣṇavism." *Wiener Zeitschrift für die Kunde Süd-und Ostasiens und Archiv für indische Philosophie*, IX (1965), 147-54.

———. "The Sānkhyization of the Emanation Doctrine Shown in a Critical Analysis of Texts." *Purāṇa*, IV (July 1962), 298-338.

Hardy, Friedhelm. *Viraha Bhakti: The Early History of Kṛṣṇa Devotion in South India.* Delhi: Oxford University Press, 1983.

Hawley, John Stratton. "Krishna's Cosmic Victories." *Journal of the American Academy of Religion*. XLVII (June 1979), 201-21.

———. *Krishna, The Butter Thief.* Princeton: Princeton University Press, 1983.

———. "Theif of Butter, Thief of Love." *History of Religions.* XVIII (Summer 1979) 203-20.

Hazra, R. C. *New Indian Antiquary*, I (November 1938), 522-28.

———. *Studies in the Puranic Records on Hindu Rites and Customs.* Delhi: Motilal Banarsidass, 1974 [1940].

Hiltebeitâl, Alf. "*Mahābhārata* and Hindu Eschatology." *History of Religions*, XII (November 1972), 95-135.

Hiriyanna, M. "The Philosophy of Bhedabheda" in *Indian Philosophical Studies I.* Mysore : Kavyalaya Publishers, 1957.

———. *Outlines of Indian Philosophy.* London: George Allen & Unwin, 1964.

Hopkins, E. Washburn. *Epic Mythology.* Delhi: Motilal Banarsidass, 1974 [1915].

Hopkins, Thomas J. *The Hindu Religious Tradition.* Belmont, Ca. : Wadsworth, 1971.

———. "The Social Teaching of the *Bhāgavata Purāna.*" *Krishna: Myths, Rites, and Attitudes.* Edited by Milton Singer. Chicago: University of Chicago Press 1968.

———. "The Vaishṇava Bhakti Movement in the *Bhāgavata Purāṇa.*" Unpublished Ph.D. dissertation, Yale University, 1961.

Hospital, Clifford G. "The Enemy Transformed : Opponents of the Lord in the *Bhāgavata Purāṇa.*" *Journal of the American Academy of Religion.* XLVI (June 1979), supplement : 200-15.

———. "Līlā in the Bhāgavata Purāṇa." *Purāṇa.* XXII (January 1980), 4-22.

Hudson, Dennis. "Bathing in Krishna." *Harvard Theological Review.* LXXVIII (January 1980), 539-66.

Ingalls, Daniel H. H. "Foreword." *Krishna : Myths, Rites and Attitudes.* Edited by Milton Singer. Chicago : University of Chicago Press, 1968.

Jaiswal, Suvira. *The Origin and Development of Vaiṣṇavism.* Delhi : Munshiram Manoharlal, 1967.

Johanns, Pierre, S. J. *A Synopsis of To Christ Through the Vedanta*. 4 vols. Ranchi : Catholic Press, 1944.

Joshi, G. N. *Atman and Moksa*. Ahmedabad : Gujarat University, 1965.

Joshi, Rasik Vihari. "Catuhsloki or Saptasloki, Bhāgavata : A Critical Study." *Purana*. XVI (January 1974), 26-46.

———. "The First Verse of Śrīmad-Bhāgavata Mahā-Purāṇa." *Purāṇa*. VI (July 1964), 378-90.

Kantawala, S. G. *Cultural History from the Matsyapurāṇa*. Baroda : Maharaja Sayajirao University of Baroda, 1964.

Kinsley, David R. *The Divine Player : A Study of Krishna-Lila*. Delhi : Motilal Banarsidass, 1979.

———. *The Sword and the Flute: Kālī and Kṛṣṇa, Dark Visions of the Terrible and the Sublime in Hindu Mythology*. Berkeley: University of California Press, 1975.

———. "Without Kṛṣṇa There is No Song." *History of Religions*, XII (November 1972), 149-80.

Kumarappa, Bharatan. *The Hindu Conception of the Deity*. London : Luzac & Co., 1934.

Lad, A. K. *A Comparative Study of the Concept of Liberation in Indian Philosophy*. Chowk : Girdharlal Keshavdas, 1967.

Larson, Gerald James. *Classical Sāṃkhya*. Delhi : Motilal Banarsidass, 1969.

Lott, Eric. *Vedantic Approaches to God*. New York : Barnes & Noble, 1980.

Macnicol, Nicol. *Indian Theism from the Vedic to the Muhammadan Period*. Delhi : Munshiram Manoharlal, 1968 [1915].

Mahadevan, T. M. P. *Outlines of Hinduism*. Bombay : Chetana, 1956.

Mani, Vettam. *Purāṇic Encyclopaedia*. Delhi : Motilal Banarsidass, 1975.

Marfatia, Mrudula. *The Philosophy of Vallabhācārya*. Delhi : Munshiram Manoharlal, 1967.

Masson, J. L. "The Childhood of Kṛṣṇa : Some Psychoanalytical Observations." *Journal of the American Oriental Society*, XCIII (1974), 454-59.

Monier-Williams, Monier. *A Sanskrit-English Dictionary*. Oxford : At the Clarendon Press, 1899.

Narain, K. *An Outline of Madhva Philosophy*. Allahabad : Udayana Publications, 1968.

Nygren, Anders. *Agape and Eros*. Translated by Philip S. Watson. Harper Torchbooks. New York : Harper & Row, 1969.

Pargiter, F. E. *Ancient Indian Historical Tradition*. London : Oxford University Press, 1922.

———. *The Purāṇa Text of the Dynasties of the Kali Age*. London : Oxford University Press, 1913.

Pereira, José. *Hindu Theology : A Reader*. Garden City, N. Y. : Doubleday, 1976.

Perrin, Norman. *What is Redaction Criticism* Philadelphia : Fortress Press, 1969.

Prasad, Shiva Shanker. "Did the Author of Bhāgavata Know Kālidāsa ?" *Purāṇa*. VI (July 1964), 378-90.

Pusalker, A. D. *Studies in Epics and Purāṇas of India*. Bombay : Bharatiya Vidya Bhavan, 1963.

Radhakrishnan, Sarvepalli., ed. *The Cultural Heritage of India*. 4 vols. Calcutta : Ramakrishna Mission Institute of Culture, 1962.

———, and Moore, Charles A. *A Sourcebook in Indian Philosophy*. Princeton : Princeton University Press, 1957.

Ramachandran, T. P. *The Indian Philosophy of Beauty*. 2 vols. Madras : University of Madras, 1979-80.

Rao, K. B. Ramakrishna. *Theism of Pre-Classical Sāṃkhya*. Mysore : University of Mysore, 1966.

Raychaudhuri, H. C. *Materials for the Study of the Early History of the Vaishṇava Sect*. New Delhi : Oriental Books Reprint Corporation, 1975 [1920].

Roy, S. N. "On the Comparative Chronology of the Vishṇu and Bhāgavata Purāṇas. *Purāṇa*. X (February 1968), 55-67.

Ruben, Walter. "The Kṛṣṇacārita in the Harivaṃśa and Certain Purāṇas." *Journal of the American Oriental Society*, LXI (1941), 115-27.

Rukmani, T. S. *A Critical Study of the Bhāgavata Purāṇa*. Chowkhamba Sanskrit Studies, Vol. LXXVII. Varanasi : Chowkhamba Sanskrit Series Office, 1970.

Sarma, B. N. Krisnamurti. "The Date of the Bhāgavata Purāṇa." *Annals of the Bhandarkar Oriental Research Institute*, XIV, 182-218.

Sastri, K. A. *The Development of Religion in South India*. Bombay : Orient Longmans, 1963.

———. *A History of South India*. London : Oxford University Press, 1958.

Sastri, P. "The Mahāpurāṇas." *Journal of the Bihar and Orissa Research Society*, XIV (1928), Part III, 323-40.

Sastri, S. Śrīkaṇṭha. "The Saviśeṣābheda Theory," in *A Volume of Eastern Studies Presented to Professor F. W. Thomas*. Edited by S. M. Katre and P. K. Gode. Bombay : Karnatak Publishing House, 1939.

Schrader, F. Otto. *Introduction to the Pāñcarātra and the Ahirbudhnya Saṃhitā*. Adyar, Madras : Adyar Library, 1916.

Sen Gupta, Anima. *Classical Samkhya : A Critical Study*. Patna : Patna University, 1969.

———. *The Evolution of the Samkhya School of Thought*. Patna : Pioneer Press, 1969.

Seshadri, K. "Viśiṣtādvaita and Identity-in-Difference." *Journal of the Philosophical Association* [India], VI (January 1959), 19-24.

Shah, Jethalal G. *Shri Vallabhacarya : His Philosophy and Religion*. Nadiad : Pushtimargiya Pustakalaya, 1961.

Sharma, B.K.N. *A History of the Dvaita School of Vedānta and Its Literature*. Bombay : Booksellers' Publishing Co., 1960.

———. *Madhva's Teaching in His Own Words*. Bombay : Bharatiya Vidya Bhavan, 1963.

———. *Philosophy of Sri Madhvacarya*. Bombay; Bharatiya Vidya Bhavan, 1962.

Sheridan, Daniel. "The Bhāgavata-purāṇa : Sāṃkhya at the Service of Non-dualism." *Purāṇa*. XXV (July 1983), 225-34.

———. "Devotion in the Bhāgavata Purāṇa and Christian Love: Bhakti, Agape, Eros." *Horizons*. VIII (Fall 1981), 260-78.

Sheridan, Daniel. "Manifestations of the Divive in the *Bhagavata Purana*." *Purana*, *XXVI* (July 12, 1984), 2, 97-112.

Shinn, Larry Dwight. "Kṛṣṇa's *Līlā* : An Analysis of the Relationship of the Notion of Deity and the Concept of *Saṃsāra* in the *Bhāgavata Purāṇa*." Unpublished Ph.D. dissertation, Princeton University, 1972.

Sinha, P.N. *A Study of the Bhagavata Purana or Esoteric Hinduism*. Adyar, Madras : Adyar Library, 1950.

Sircar, D.C., ed. *The Bhakti Cult and Ancient Indian Geography*. Calcutta : University of Calcutta, 1970.

———. *Studies in the Religious Life of Ancient and Medieval India*. Delhi : Motilal Banarsidass, 1971.

Spink, Walter M. *Krishnamandala* : *A Devotional Theme in Indian Art*. Ann Arbor : Center for South and Southeast Asian Studies, 1971.

Srinivasachari, P. N. *The Philosophy of Bhedābheda*. Madras : Adyar Library and Research Center, 1972.

Vaidya, C.V. "The Date of the *Bhāgavata Purāṇa*." *Journal of the Bombay Branch of the Royal Asiatic Society*, New Series, I (1925), 145-58.

van Buitenen, J.A.B. "On the Archaism of the *Bhāgavata Puraṇa*." *Krishna* : *Myths, Rites, and Attitudes*. Edited by Milton Singer. Chicago : University of Chicago Press, 1968.

Varadachari, K. C. *Alvars of South India*. Bombay : Bharatiya Vidya Bhavan, 1966.

Vaudeville, Ch. "Evolution of Love-Symbolism in Bhagavatism." *Journal of the American Oriental Society*, LXXXII (March 1962), 31-40.

Walker, Benjamin. *Hindu World* : *An Encyclopedic Survey of Hinduism*. 2 vols. London : George Allen & Unwin, 1968.

White, Charles. "Kṛṣṇa as Divine Child." *History of Religions*, X (November 1970), 156-77.

Wilson, H. H. *Essays Analytical, Critical and Philological*. London : Trubner & Co., 1864-1865.

Winternitz, Moriz. *A History of Indian Literature*. Translated by S. Ketkar. 2 vols. New York : Russell & Russell, 1971.

Yocum, Glenn. "Shrines, Shamanism, and Love Poetry : Elements in the Emergence of Popular Tamil Bhakti." *Journal of the American Academy of Religion*, XLI (March 1973), 3-17.

INDEX OF TEXTS CITED AND QUOTED

Bhāgavata Purāṇa (*indicates citation without quotation)

INDEX OF NAMES AND TEXTS

INDEX OF SUBJECTS

(includes personalities found in the *Bhāgavata Purāṇa*)

ERRATA

Page		line 32	For "Witernitz", read "Winternitz".
Page	6	line 37	For "Bhakati", read "Bhakti".
Page	6	line 37	For "Bhāgavata", read "*Bhāgavata*".
Page	8	line 30	For "againt", read "against".
Page	20	line 6	Add period after plurality.
Page	20	line 38	For "maith", read "matiḥ".
Page	22	line 29	For "jivalo", read "jīvalo".
Page	23	line 28	For "With", read "Without".
Page	24	line 32	For "vaśuddhaṃ", read "viśuddhaṃ".
Page	28	line 35	For "putrasnehamayiṃ", read "putrasnehamayīṃ".
Page	35	line 16	For "somthing", read "something".
Page	37	line 7	For "Vesudeva", read "Vasudeva".
Page	45	line 6	For "in", read "In".
Page	54	line 17	For "A", read "As".
Page	57	line 25	For "Journey", read "journey".
Page	59	line 32	For "ṚV", read "Ṛg".
Page	61	line 38	For "I.3.18a", read "I.3.28a".
Page	64	line 5	For "Vasudeva", read "Vāsudeva".
Page	64	line 37	For "III.26.21, 95, 28", read "III.26.21, 25, 28".
Page	73	line 23	For "conto", read "canto".
Page	74	line 7	For "Bhgavān", read "Bhagavān".
Page	81	line 2	For "is all the human", read "is the human".
Page	85	line 26	For "tradition", read "traditions".
Page	94	line 4	For "lead", read "leads".
Page	95	line 9	For "datachment", read "detachment".
Page	124	line 37	For "Atman and Moksa", read "Ātman and Mokṣa".
Page	144	line 8	For "and", read "an".
Page	147	line 39	For "non-entity", read "non-reality".

Page 151	line 4	Add *The Bhāgavata Purāṇa*. Translated by Ganesh Vasudeo Tagare. 5 vols. Delhi : Motilal Banarsidass, 1976-1978.
Page 155	line 1	For "Theif", read "Thief".
Page 159	line 1	For "Divive", read "Divine".